Bobcat

FIFTY YEARS OF OPPORTUNITY

1958–2008

MARTY PADGETT

First published in 2007 by Motorbooks, an imprint of MBI Publishing Company LLC, Galtier Plaza, Suite 200, 380 Jackson Street, St. Paul, MN 55101 USA

Motorbooks titles are also available at discounts in bulk quantity for industrial or sales-promotional use. For details write to Special Sales Manager at MBI Publishing Company, Galtier Plaza, Suite 200, 380 Jackson Street, St. Paul, MN 55101 USA.

To find out more about our books, join us online at www.motorbooks.com.

On the cover: The machine that changed the world by giving one man the strength of ten.

On the frontispiece: A European version M600 at work on a jobsite. Featuring a four-cylinder Wisconsin VH4D engine, the M600 was built between 1967 and 1975.

On the title pages: At one point—with Bobcat owning 50 percent of the global skid-steer loader market, the popular 743 model made up half of all Bobcat loaders shipped, which meant a quarter of the skid-steers being sold worldwide were 743s. *(left)* The Beginning: Here, an early Melroe M60 self-propelled three-wheeled loader transports a bucket of dirt. *(right)* Today: This Bobcat T320 compact track loader hauling a pallet of bricks represents the new generation of Bobcat loaders.

On the back cover: *(above)* A semitrailer transports a shipment of new Bobcat loaders that will soon find themselves in the hands of customers all across the country and overseas.
(lower right) The M610 (left) and the B-Series 520 (1976) both retain the characteristic orange tailgate, though the 520's is significantly different, for easier engine access.

About the Author: Marty Padgett has been an automotive journalist since the 1990s. He is currently editor of "the Web's automotive authority," TheCarConnection.com. In addition, Padgett contributes regularly to *Stuff* magazine as its resident "road warrior." He also writes car news and columns for *Import Tuner*, Edmunds.com, and other publications. Over the years, his articles have appeared in a wide range of magazines, including *Car and Driver*, *Outside*, *AutoWeek*, *Men's Health*, and *Details*.

ISBN-13: 978-0-7603-3212-2

Editor: James Michels
Designer: Brenda C. Canales

Printed in China

Contents

	FOREWORD	6
Chapter 1	**BORN ON THE FARM**	8
Chapter 2	**BOBCAT COMES OF AGE**	32
Chapter 3	**INVENTION AND INNOVATION (1969—1983)**	80
Chapter 4	**LET THE GAMES BEGIN**	120
Chapter 5	**LEADER OF THE PACK**	144
Chapter 6	**MARKETING HISTORY**	186
Chapter 7	**REFLECTIONS**	198
Chapter 8	**BOBCAT LORE**	204
Chapter 9	**DEALER CHANNEL**	210
Chapter 10	**SALES MEETINGS**	219
Chapter 11	**BOBCAT OH, THE PLACES WE'VE BEEN . . .**	229
	PRODUCT INDEX	232
	ACKNOWLEDGEMENTS	260
	EPILOGUE	261
	INDEX	262

Foreword

Bobcat Company Historian

Leroy Anderson

It's been a half century since a small manufacturer in southeastern North Dakota and two blacksmith-inventor brothers from west central Minnesota joined forces to build a machine that would change the world. One wonders what might have been had brothers Les, Cliff, Roger and Irv Melroe—of the Melroe Manufacturing Company—not come across Cyril and Louis Keller and their three-wheeled loader that could turn within its own length. Or had farmer Eddie Velo not stopped by the Kellers' blacksmith shop to grumble about the difficulty in cleaning out turkey barns. What if the Kellers had not devised a solution for Velo? What if the Melroes hadn't invited the Kellers to demonstrate their machine at the 1958 Minnesota State Fair?

The account of how these remarkable businessmen and innovators crossed paths and eventually began working together has its share of entrepreneurial vision, good fortune, and timing. But as the success story continues to unfold, leadership, perseverance, and ingenuity reach an entirely new scale: the Melroe Manufacturing Company puts a small North Dakota town on the map, lives are changed, and the bar for technology is set and continually raised. At the same time, manufacturers all over the world begin to chase the pioneer of the skid-steer loader, which the Melroes designated "Bobcat" in 1962 because of its toughness, quickness, and agility.

How the Machine that Changed the World EVOLVED

Keller Loader
1957

M60
1958

M200
1959

M400
1960

6

Well, others are still chasing that nimble animal today. But after the Melroe Manufacturing Company was acquired by Clark Equipment Company, and then Clark was subsequently acquired by Ingersoll-Rand Company, the name "Bobcat" has come to represent much more than just skid-steer loaders. Bobcat Company is the world leader in the design, manufacture, marketing, and distribution of compact equipment, with a range of skid-steer loaders, compact track loaders, compact excavators (the only brand manufactured in the United States), mini track loaders, telescopic tool carriers, utility vehicles, and attachments. "Bobcat" no longer refers exclusively to a machine; it has become a powerful global brand.

Over the years, thousands of individuals have contributed to the Melroe and Keller legacies, helping Bobcat become what it is today. You will see the word "opportunity" throughout this book. The Keller loader, the Melroe Manufacturing Company, Clark Equipment Company, Ingersoll-Rand Company, and Bobcat Company have given thousands of individuals the opportunity to enjoy quality jobs close to home, excel as professionals, become leaders, and be part of a genuine success story—one that will be remembered for decades to come. This book is a tribute to them . . . the Bobcat story.

M440
1962

M600 Electric
1968

M970
1970

M371
1971

M610
1972

825
1975

632
1977

743
1981

753
1990

7753
1991

S185
2002

S330
2006

>> Ed Larson, Melroe employee, says he was charged with breaking the company's new machines "so we could find out and fix it before it went to the customer." Here Larson clears snow in an M400 in Gwinner, North Dakota.

① Born on the Farm

There are certain things men will always do better than machines, like building violins and delivering babies and dancing. But a machine's ability to free us from laborious tasks by exerting forces several or even dozens of men together could not exceed has long established its permanence in modern society. Motorized, hydraulic, electric, computerized—devices allow us to move and create at speeds and magnitudes we can only match in our imaginations. And, every so often, a single machine transforms a whole industry, rendering prior methods obsolete.

The power of America lies in its power to innovate. America has born and bred some of the globe's most important technologies, from the cotton gin to the Internet. Harnessing the power of machines was at the core of the American revolution that transformed the nation from a rural agrarian society into an urban, technically sophisticated global leader. At its birth, America sustained itself; through its ingenuity and know-how, America today helps sustain the world.

The Bobcat story—the machines, the company, the people—is one of thousands of examples of the technology that grew up in America and changed the world. But it's a unique tale. From its farmland beginnings to its modern-day iconic status, Bobcat machines of all kinds—and separately, but integrally, the skid-steer loader itself—are stories of innovation. Pioneers cultivating North Dakota grain fields

>> *E. G. (Edward Gideon) Melroe is known as the grandfather of the Bobcat loader, and as his biography* E. G.–Inventor by Necessity *retells, his was an ongoing story of innovation in agriculture.*

9

saw potential in an idea from neighboring Minnesota, made it more robust, then unleashed it on a country that happened to be in the beginning of a massive transformation from farmscape to cityscape.

The Bobcat skid-steer loader arose from the need for a new kind of machine, one that would facilitate this change by making manual labor easier. It would free workers to be more efficient, turning the power of one man into the power

>> It was the combine that got the Melroe family into the farm implement business. E. G. Melroe bought one of the first combines in North Dakota in 1927 and operates this one, a Case Model P. The combine and the windrow pickup he invented are now on display at the Bonanzaville museum, in West Fargo, North Dakota.

>> Before E. G. Melroe passed away in 1955, he had pioneered the two inventions that underwrote the development of the skid-steer loader. Though the company later sold off its windrow pickup and harroweeder businesses, the products made the Melroe Manufacturing Company enough money to take an interest in the three-wheel loader being built by the Keller brothers in the late 1950s.

of many. By doing so, it would change the face of the nation.

And it all began in the Midwest, the vast interior of America that's not often commemorated in music or television or in popular culture, but which feeds and fosters us all. Today, around the world, Bobcat compact machines are icons of American ingenuity—whether they're in action preparing Beijing for the 2008 Summer Olympics, or on a turkey farm in Arkansas preparing the barn for a new shipment of toms.

But its earliest roots lead back to the first half of the twentieth century, when a few sharp minds turned the idea of farm machinery around in their heads until they turned the whole idea of farm machinery on its own head. And, by the time President John F. Kennedy promised a man would land on the moon, the men at the heart of the Bobcat revolution— Eddie Velo, Louis and Cyril Keller, and the Melroe brothers— had conceived a machine that would become known worldwide by the brand name "Bobcat."

What follows is a story of innovation and ingenuity, of resilience and self-reliance, of the ability to recognize weakness and to capitalize on strength. What follows is a story of the American dream.

MELROE'S EARLY DAYS

"If E. G. Melroe inherited any outstanding traits from his parents, it was his obdurate resolve to see a job through," wrote Robert Karolevitz, author of E. G. Melroe's biography, *E. G. - Inventor by Necessity*.

Edward Gideon Melroe, or E. G. as he was also known, was one of the pioneers in agricultural technology in the era before World War II. Described by contemporaries and family as an inventive man, he grew up on the plains of North Dakota, in the tiny town of Gwinner, about 90 miles southwest of Fargo.

Gwinner was one of hundreds of rural towns dotting the Upper Midwest that were devoted to farming, with families tilling large tracts of black, fertile earth to grow crops like hard red spring wheat, North Dakota's signature product. With fewer than 300 full-time residents, Gwinner's ties to the 39th state's larger towns—Fargo and Bismarck—were distant at best. North Dakota itself, only having been a state for a generation, counted about half a million citizens— nearly as many as it does today—and still held firmly to its place in the Wild West.

Melroe's family sent him to the North Dakota Agricultural College in Fargo. This tenure in school implanted the notion of mechanizing farm life in the young man, and when he returned to his family's acreage, Melroe began converting some of the farm's manual labor to machine-driven modernity, first with a tractor, then with a corn binder (a device that cuts corn stalks and binds them in bundles).

During the Depression, Melroe refined his mechanical abilities out of necessity, rebuilding broken farm equipment because replacing it was out of the question. By mechanizing where he could, and by keeping those machines running properly, he increased the size of his farm—expanding from 480 to 3,500 acres by the end of the 1930s. With his inventive mind, and education in steam- and gas-powered machines, Melroe saw room for more than repairs in available farm equipment. He knew he could improve it, bettering not only his own farm but farming itself.

As droughts and economic difficulties leading up to the Great Depression hobbled farming communities in the late 1920s, Melroe saw that agriculture's future lay in more efficient production. And that required machines. So in 1927, E. G. Melroe and his brother, Sig, became the first combine owners in the state of North Dakota. Until the combine was invented, farmers used binders to cut grain, then stacked it in shocks to be threshed later. Combines were the first effective way to cut the grain and feed it into a threshing machine in a single operation.

In 1928, the harvest season was interrupted by several days of rain. With the rain came pigeon grass and other weeds that intermingled with the standing grain. These green weeds proved to be too tough for the threshing mechanism of their combine, so E. G. converted a binder into a swather that laid the grain out for drying, curing, and easier threshing.

Next, Melroe ordered a pickup attachment from an agricultural machine manufacturer in California. But it didn't do the job as well as they expected, so E. G. made some changes, improving it enough to finally harvest the crop. After two years, Melroe abandoned that pickup attachment and

>> *The Melroe Manufacturing Company's harroweeder had some notable distinctions over the harroweeder of the day. The most important was the "electro-tempered" steel, engineered with U.S. Steel, which gave the Melroe harrow the ability to cull weeds while it cultivated the soil.*

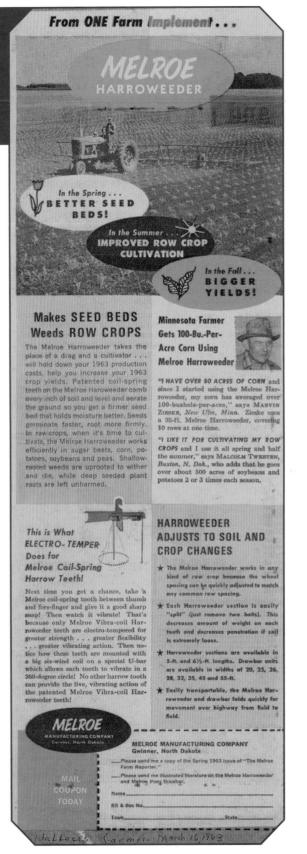

11

>> High school and college students—including the Melroe brothers—would work after school and summers, placing the staples during the pickup assembly process.

>> This early photo of the Melroe windrow pickup shows the aluminum apron that had to be pieced together by hand.

built one of his own design. Using belts from an old muck elevator, he created an apron upon which he attached the teeth, or fingers, that gathered and lifted the grain onto the threshing platform. The rollers came from a worn-out binder, and the frame was a cut-down auto chassis.

The result was the windrow pickup. As he refined his design, Melroe brought in his sons—Lester, Clifford, Roger, and Irving—as assembly hands. Together, they produced a small number of windrow pickups for their own farm and for neighboring farms. Three pickups were built in 1937 and twelve in 1938.

Cliff recalled that building the pickups took most of his and his brothers' spare time. Ranging in age from 12 to 20, the Melroe boys cut the pickups' teeth from rolls of wire and helped put everything together. "We drilled the holes with hand drills and tightened nuts and bolts with pliers and wrenches," said Cliff. During the school year, the brothers and their sister, Evelyn, rode to and from school in a horse-drawn buggy. When they got back home, the brothers worked the

>> Melroe advertised its windrow pickup as the most effective way to get the most from a bushel of grain. "Lifts the windrow carefully . . . to save every kernel! Picks cleaner . . . gets more grain," this ad promised.

>> This photo shows how the Melroe windrow pickup lifted windrows of grain.

farm and built more pickups—with some time spared for baseball, an avid pastime. Through it all, Evelyn, who everyone called Evie, and the matriarch of the Melroe clan, Mabel, kept everyone well fed.

Melroe continued to tinker with, and to refine, his windrow pickup. But in 1939, the 47-year-old farmer suffered a heart attack at a church outing. Then a blood clot settled in his right leg, requiring amputation. To cover his medical bills, Melroe sold the windrow pickup patent rights to the John Deere Company for $5,000.

"I felt in my mind that E. G. became a manager after he lost the leg," recalls Gene Dahl, the husband of daughter Evie, and later a director of the Melroe Manufacturing Company. "He had to go around with crutches, then he could get by on a cane."

His medical bills paid, Melroe kept working on refining the windrow pickup, outfitting it with a sort of independent suspension that allowed it to keep the apron closer to the ground, making it even more efficient, and revamping the apron and its metal teeth for better action.

MELROE MANUFACTURING IS BORN

After selling his patent to John Deere, E. G.'s creative mind told him there had to be a better way of handling the grain after it was stacked in windrows. He settled on aluminum slats stapled to fabric belts. The secret of his resulting invention was the way the teeth picked the grain up from the ground and laid it on the canvas belt that would then take it to the threshing cylinder.

This was accomplished by the bottom roller being somewhat smaller in diameter than the top roller. As the pickup tooth came around the bottom roller, the tooth caught on the aluminum slat and became rigid. As the tooth came over the top roller, the larger diameter of that roller caused the tooth to release, allowing the grain to lay down for a low delivery to the auger. This pickup quickly developed a reputation for having

>> *Upon his sons' safe return from the war, E. G. Melroe formed the Melroe Manufacturing Company in 1947 as the parent company for the windrow pickup. E.G Melroe (foreground) is pictured here with his four sons (left to right): Roger, Lester, Irving, and Clifford.*

the best picking action of anything on the market—even better than the idea Melroe had sold to John Deere.

When World War II started, three of Melroe's sons—Roger, Lester and Irving—went off to fight. Melroe decided to move the pickup operation from the farm into "downtown" Gwinner, where it might be easier to hire some help. He bought an empty gas station and set up a new workshop and facility for the pickup, while son Clifford helped to manage the family farm—which by the day's standards was "monstrous," according to Melroe's biographer.

Upon his sons' safe return from the war, Melroe formed the Melroe Manufacturing Company in 1947 as the parent company for the pickup. With his sons again working at his side, he moved production from the former gas station site to

a vacant schoolhouse, but even at that facility it soon became clear that the Melroe Manufacturing production line would require more space. After purchasing a used punch press, a drill press, and a turning lathe in 1948, E. G. Melroe took heed of his young sons and paid to construct a 100-by-30-foot factory building.

Within a year, the Melroes added onto that building, and boosted their payroll to 10 employees. They leased out the family farm, since the brothers were busy hauling concrete blocks for the Melroe factory's construction.

With E. G. at the helm, and Cliff Melroe helping with engineering, the remaining brothers focused their efforts on selling windrow pickups throughout the spring and summer.

THE MELROE HARROWEEDER

E. G. Melroe's windrow pickup quickly became a strong seller for his young company. Though he continued to refine it, the machine's future fell to his sons when E. G. died in 1955.

In the early 1950s, E. G. Melroe had an idea on how to improve the harrow. Harrows are used after fields are plowed to break up large clumps of dirt into a finer soil mix. But until then, harrows were simple machines without flexible teeth, and they would often break in hard soil. Melroe studied existing designs before coming up with his own—and in doing so, gave the Melroe Manufacturing Company its second home-grown farming implement.

Melroe's idea was to use coil springs for the harrow. By using springs, the device would gently stir the soil, separating bigger chunks of earth and settling finer dirt below them into a moist bed—ideal for growing grain crops. The harrow also turned out to be a good implement for killing weeds—it pulled smaller plants with shallow roots while leaving the deeper roots of plants like corn, soybeans and beets intact.

Though he had no formal training in metallurgy, Melroe knew the design would require a special metal coil. The company called on U.S. Steel's expertise to come up with a coil spring design that would have a long, useful life. And by 1959, the tempering process for the metal used in the coil springs was perfected.

The harroweeder was born. It was capable of cultivating 16 or 24 rows of corn, taking 55-foot passes. And it gave Melroe Manufacturing a second important product, the sales of which generated the cash needed to develop the company's new products.

>> *E.G Melroe's company first built the windrow pickup. Its second successful product, the harroweeder, used strong, flexible steel coils to prepare the ground for planting while also weeding out rows of corn, soybeans, and beets. Brother Ted Melroe is on the left.*

>> As farms grew larger, farmers needed larger equipment. Thanks to the inventions of E. G. Melroe, farmers today are able to use extra-wide windrow pickups like this one, capable of collecting two windrows at a time.

>> The first dedicated Melroe Manufacturing Company factory followed two smaller facilities—an old gas station, then a vacant schoolhouse. E. G. Melroe stands outside the company factory in Gwinner, North Dakota, in 1948.

In the winter, the family worked on the assembly line, adding Gene Dahl to the ranks in 1950. Irving Melroe recalled those early days, when he went from farm to farm and to implement dealers trying to sell their product. "[I] felt like a country bumpkin going to town with a basket of eggs to sell," he said, "except, you didn't have to explain an egg to every buyer."

Because the start-up business was selling new ideas, times weren't always easy—and nature rarely complied. The 1950s were a period of struggle for the young company, which never had the cashflow to develop new products. Lean finances were aggravated by reliance on the weather and crops. A wheat rust epidemic in 1953 ruined crops across the region, leading to canceled orders and a financial crisis at Melroe Manufacturing. Although the company's pickup inventory was sold on paper, money had yet to change hands—and the machines remained locked in Melroe's warehouse facility.

As the brothers considered closing down Melroe Manufacturing, the company got into a dispute with Reynolds Aluminum over payment for a shipment of materials. According to E. G.'s biographer, Reynolds' credit manager called the Melroes, reaching Roger. "I'm sorry, but our representative had no authorization for extending credit," said the voice from Chicago. "You'll either have to pay or we'll be forced to take some sort of action against you." There was a silence. Roger had no response. Then the Reynolds man continued, "In looking over your records, it seems to me that your company is an excellent risk. You show no credit defaults or other indications of unsound operation. Somebody should be willing to take a chance on you." He suggested they talk to the First National Bank of Chicago and offered to make the proper introductions. The company ended up brokering a business-saving credit deal.

The biggest challenge for the young company came in 1955 when its founder passed away. E. G. Melroe had started the company and invented its chief products, the windrow pickup and a harroweeder with a unique spring-coil design. Now, the brothers would have to step in and take charge. They divided up duties at the company, naming Clifford president, Roger secretary-treasurer, and Lester, Irving, and brother-in-law Eugene Dahl vice presidents.

The company they inherited was built from the farm up, essentially selling to other farmers through implement dealers. "We had combined a lot more grain and tilled a lot more ground than most dealers," Roger Melroe wrote of the company's time in transition. "And whenever some of the machines wouldn't work, we would go out in the field and fix them ourselves."

The Melroes were farmers who sold farm machines to other farmers. Yet their future and their company's lay on a different path, one they would chart with another set of brothers. The two families met by chance in Rothsay, Minnesota, during the summer of 1958. By that same chance was set the foundation for a new machine—one that would change Melroe Manufacturing Company from farm equipment maker into compact machine empire.

FATHERS OF INVENTION

"I'd say you're born with some knowledge," believes Cyril Keller. *"Everybody has a gift. I can't play a piano, but if you [want me to] get a piece of metal and make something, I can do it."*

The Keller brothers, like the Melroes, came from farming backgrounds. In Rothsay, Minnesota, Louis and Cyril Keller ran a blacksmith shop that served the local farm community by remanufacturing plowshares and fixing other iron implements. According to the Keller brothers' descendants, Louis opened the shop in 1947 and ran it himself until about 1953, when Cyril joined the business.

"Louis had more work than he could handle," Cyril recalled. "The big business was making wagons for farmers using parts from old cars—Plymouth cars," he said.

Plowshare work was a major part of the Rothsay shop's business. "We were taking two old plowshares and making [them into] one for farmers," Cyril said. "In the winter, we'd take the plowshares, especially for John Deere and International models, and we would make [our own]." If a farmer wanted a set, Keller remembered, "he had to bring two sets in and pay the difference. We would guarantee they would outlast a new plowshare." The Kellers' secret was tempered steel, which would last far longer than what local farmers were accustomed to.

Though Louis had the reputation as the inventor and engineer of the pair, both worked on devices that were later sold to other companies. An example was a ribbon-auger

>> *Like the Melroes, Louis Keller (left) and Cyril Keller came from farming backgrounds. Though Louis had the reputation as the inventor and engineer of the pair, both worked on devices that were later sold to other companies.*

>> *The Kellers' blacksmith shop in Rothsay, Minnesota, later became Keller Manufacturing when the brothers began building three-wheel loaders. When the Kellers joined Melroe Manufacturing Company, friend Ed Schillinger was left to run the business for 18 months until it was sold.*

EDDIE VELO AND THE KELLER LOADER

Eddie Velo's offhand wish for an easier way to clean up his farm was all it took to launch the fifty-year history of the Bobcat skid-steer loader. And while instigator isn't the right word for the Minnesota turkey farmer, certainly without his need for a new way of doing business, the machine would never have been built.

Velo was born in October 1909 near Rothsay, Minnesota. Married to his wife Leola, Velo became an important figure in agriculture and farming even before the three-wheeled loader, as one of the first in his area to see the potential in larger operations—the future of agribusiness. He was president and a founder of West Central Turkeys Inc., of Pelican Rapids.

But the bigger operation Velo presided over presented a problem: he needed a way to clean out his massive two-story turkey barns faster than a man with a shovel and wheelbarrow could manage. He turned to the Kellers with his problems and possibly had the idea for a rear caster-wheel loader.

"I knew him well," said Dale Western, former copywriter for Bobcat's advertising agency.

It was Velo's original needs that laid out the engineering requirements for the first Keller loader. It had to be nimble—able to navigate around poles set eight feet apart. It had to be able to turn, scrape, and dump with a bucket or fork. And it had to be reliable.

Velo's requirements resulted in the Keller loader, and later the Melroe Self-Propelled loaders. So convinced by the Keller's first attempt at a loader was Velo that he wrote them a testimonial: "In my operation, I consider this machine so valuable that I wouldn't sell it for any price," Velo wrote in 1958.

But when it came to the skid-steer principle, Velo wasn't sold on the idea of adding extra wheels to the basic loader. "Eddie, when he saw that four-wheel thing, I'm sure he said 'that thing won't be any good, it doesn't swivel!'" Western said. "You'd be putting on tires every three or six months, he thought, but it didn't work out that way."

Velo lived to see his inspiration come full circle. He died in February 1999, but his descendants live in the Fergus Falls, Minnesota, area—the home of the very first loader, which now sits on display in the Otter Tail County Museum in Fergus Falls.

18

>> *Turkey farmer Eddie Velo from Rothsay, Minnesota, is seated on the original Keller self-propelled loader.*

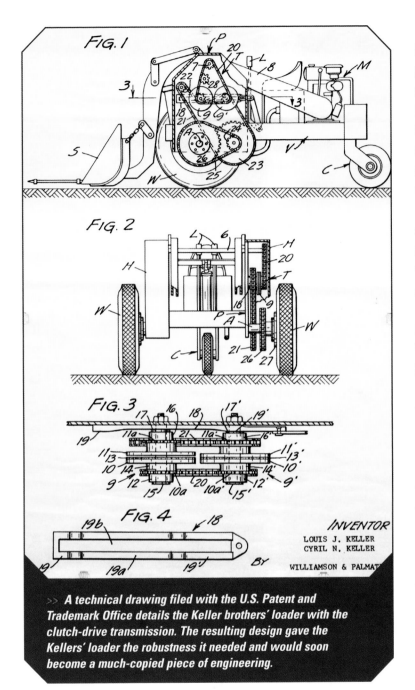

FIG. 1
FIG. 2
FIG. 3
FIG. 4

INVENTOR
LOUIS J. KELLER
CYRIL N. KELLER

BY
WILLIAMSON & PALMAT

>> *A technical drawing filed with the U.S. Patent and Trademark Office details the Keller brothers' loader with the clutch-drive transmission. The resulting design gave the Kellers' loader the robustness it needed and would soon become a much-copied piece of engineering.*

A local farmer, Eddie Velo, had a quandary in his turkey barns. He was in the process of becoming a large-scale producer, but his ever-larger barns weren't getting cleaned quickly enough using a man, a pitchfork and a wheelbarrow. He wanted to mechanize the task, yet the poles supporting the barns' roofs were only eight feet apart—too narrow for maneuvering a tractor and cart. The problem became knottier, as Velo's turkey barns had second floors—and no machine was light enough to be lifted up to the second floor.

In the summer of 1956, Velo came to the Kellers "kind of disgusted because he didn't get his barns completely clean," recalled Cyril Keller. "When his new young turkeys arrived at the barn, he had to put straw over manure he didn't get out. And he had to do it by hand."

Velo left without saying more. But the Keller brothers latched onto the problem and began working out a solution. Where a traditional tractor loader would not fit or proved too heavy, a lightweight, maneuverable machine would do the trick.

"We started thinking about that," Keller says. "We tried to figure out how we could make something that would turn in its own length."

The process of creation took them through a few scenarios. If the machine steered by turning its wheels, it would still make a loop—it wouldn't turn in its tracks. The key, they decided, was to move one side of the machine back and one side forward, so the machine would pivot on its center. A set of pulleys and belts would manage the machine's power.

With the concept in mind, the Kellers struck a deal with Velo. If their concept worked, Velo would pay a fair manufacturing cost for the resulting machine. If not, Velo would simply pay for the materials and the Kellers would be out their time. As they did with their repair business, the Kellers scoured junkyards for various pieces they needed: a caster wheel; two drive wheels; control levers for both sides of the machine. A 5-horsepower engine with a rope starter would supply the power.

To give the machine its barn-cleaning capabilities, the Kellers outfitted the new loader with 5/8-inch steel rods to tear out the accumulated manure. But initial passes with the prototype revealed those rods to be too soft for the job. "We brought it back to the shop, took the rods out, and a local cop came in and saw us taking those out," Cyril Keller said. The officer told the brothers, "I'm going to get some rods—you

snowblower that was produced in the late 1950s in Rothsay. The Farmhand company was going to put the design into mass production, but trouble with patent filings ended the relationship. An effective snowblower in northern Minnesota would have been a bankable device. But even bigger things lay ahead for the inventive brothers. The one that would change their lives and futures came to them in humble guise—as one of their neighbor's problems.

>> *Before their meeting with the Melroe brothers, the Kellers began to market their loader in western Minnesota. This piece of literature shows a brand-new kind of machine, one that was new, fast, rugged, different, compact, dependable, economical, and maneuverable. The Keller loader had it all.*

>> *Here the Keller clutch-drive transmission on the original loader is visible after removing the machine's side cover. The new clutch-drive transmission proved durable, and after February 4, 1957, the Kellers began producing loaders.*

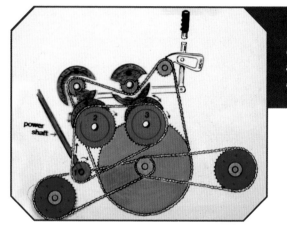

>> *An early clutch-drive system illustration.*

can't bend 'em." He came back with bars out of the old jail—"and you couldn't bend 'em," Keller laughed.

After months of effort, the Kellers delivered the first loader to Eddie Velo, who put it to immediate use. The Kellers observed his work, so that they could make running improvements to the design where needed.

The first flaw with the device made itself apparent early. The pulley-drive transmission system was prone to failure. It was hard to operate, according to the Kellers' accounts, and the belt often slipped off the pulley, leading to a complete loss

of directional control. A new design was required—and the Kellers went back to their drawing boards.

The resulting design gave their loader the robustness it needed, and would soon become a much-copied piece of engineering. The new transmission incorporated a pair of clutches governed by a tapered wedge that engaged them, connected by a chain that could reverse the direction of one of the clutches to give the machine forward and reverse locomotion to the right- and left-side wheels independently of one another. Some of the design was derived from contemporary swathers, while other parts, like the planetary principle that led to the clutch design, were also found in machines like the Ford Model T.

The new clutch-drive transmission proved durable, and after February 4, 1957, the Kellers began producing loaders.

They built six, all powered by a 6.6-horsepower Kohler engine. All were sold to poultry farms.

MELROES MOVE IN

The Kellers' machine solved a widespread problem and solved it well. They saw the potential in their new machine, but Cyril and Louis didn't have the means to mass-produce the loader they had built in series for Eddie Velo and six other customers. Rothsay's small bank could only offer a portion of the estimated $250,000 needed to set up a factory. Investors from nearby Fergus Falls showed interest, but wanted to oversee the business. The Kellers kept looking.

Their uncle, Anton Christianson, sold farm implements in Elbow Lake, Minnesota, not far from the brothers' Rothsay shop. One day in 1958, Les Melroe visited Christianson on a sales call. The men got to talking, and the latter suggested they go see what his nephews were working on in their shop. On that warm, humid August day, Les Melroe met the Kellers as they were working to replace the pulleys in Eddie Velo's loader with the clutch drive system.

"Man, he got excited about it," said Cyril Keller. Les Melroe immediately saw potential in the loader—so much so that he offered the Kellers a spot in the Melroe Manufacturing booth at the 1958 Minnesota State Fair in St. Paul. Melroe's thoughts were clearly on incorporating the loader into his company's lineup. "If you bring that to the state fair in St. Paul, put it on the lot and show it," Keller recalled Melroe telling him, "the public is going to tell us if we want to take it or not."

>> *Pictured above is the actual loader that Louis and Cyril Keller showcased in the Melroe Manufacturing booth at the 1958 Minnesota State Fair.*

The Kellers brought the loader to the Melroe booth. It was an unqualified hit with fairgoers, who gathered to watch the machine scoop up dirt and load it into a pickup. One brother would run the machine, another would pass out literature. "You'd start running it, and within a half-hour you had so many people trying to get to it, they were crowding into you," Keller said. "We stopped, shut the machine off. We were handing out as much literature as we could."

At the same time the Melroes were assessing the machine from a distance. Les Melroe was sitting up on a combine, trying to count the number of people crowding the booth in groups of 100. The other brothers would mingle in the crowd asking what customers would do with a machine like the loader on display. The answers were many and varied: farming, construction, working fertilizer plants, cleaning chicken barns.

The Melroes were sold. By the third day of the fair, Les Melroe had returned to the booth with decals in hand, putting them on the machine. "When people want something  this bad," Keller quoted him, "Melroe is going to have it."

With such an enthusiastic response to the loader, the Kellers and the Melroes struck a deal. The Kellers would come to Gwinner, North Dakota, to work for the Melroe Manufacturing Company, charged with developing the machine further. Melroe would pay a royalty to the Kellers for each loader built. In the fall of 1958, Cyril and Louis Keller rented an apartment in Gwinner to continue developing what would be named the Melroe Self-Propelled Loader. They left their blacksmith shop in the hands of family friend, Eddie Schillinger, who ran it for the next 18 months until it was sold.

IMPROVING THE BREED

The basics for the Melroe loader's drive system had been settled, but the loader needed additional engineering and development before it could be mass-produced. And since Melroe employees were already occupied making windrow pickups and harroweeders, the Kellers—with some help from Melroe engineers—built more loaders with caster wheels and clutch drive systems.

>> The M200 could be outfitted with a range of attachments, from buckets to forks to angle brooms like this one. The attachment business would later become a large part of the Bobcat business.

>> The M200 entered production in Gwinner, North Dakota, with a 12.9-hp engine and a three-wheel configuration. Here the loader is painted red and yellow, a paint scheme similar to the Farmhand brand of implements. Some early loaders were, in fact, distributed through Farmhand dealers.

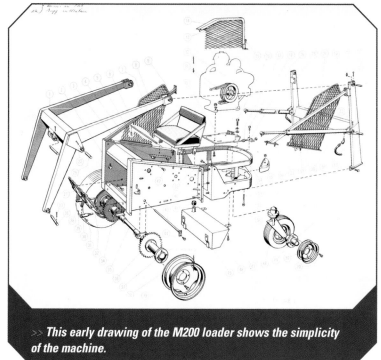

>> This early drawing of the M200 loader shows the simplicity of the machine.

The first M60 Melroe Self-Propelled Loader was quickly succeeded by an improved version with more cast-iron pieces and an updated, 12.9-horsepower two-cylinder engine made by Onan. With more technical developments and a fresh red-and-yellow paint job, the Melroe M200 was born, sporting yellow lift arms and a Melroe oval logo.

But despite all the improvements, the M200 still lacked the heavy-duty capability that customers were seeking. For poultry barns, the low-capacity Keller loader had been ideal; but with notions of using the loader in construction and heavy agriculture, the machine simply wasn't strong or stable enough to handle the load.

The Kellers and the Melroes pressed ahead with improvements, taking heed of the example E. G. Melroe had set with his windrow pickup years earlier. "You don't just start building a Bobcat loader or a combine pickup," Irving Melroe said. "Dad started things and improved on them for years before they were manufactured."

The major improvement that was needed, all the brothers agreed, was an extra pair of wheels. Syl Melroe, cousin of the Melroe brothers, came to work for the company as it faced a watershed decision—whether to continue with the loaders in some modified form of its current design, or to forge ahead with a new four-wheel design.

"The two-wheel machine, because you couldn't get enough torque or power on anything to hurt anything, it didn't break down," Syl remembered. "Consequently, you couldn't do a lot of work with it, either."

In December 1960, Cyril Keller returned from a demonstration outside of Mobridge, South Dakota, and he was discouraged. The demonstration took place in a barn where manure needed to be removed. Keller put the loader's bucket down, the front wheels rose off the ground, and the machine lost traction.

Customers encountered other problems as they put the loader to work—some uses intended by the inventors, some not anticipated in their wildest dreams. The caster wheel on the rear of the M200 would get gummed up or plugged up when the machine was used to clean dirty barns. And as Keller experienced in South Dakota, the machine didn't have the traction to push very heavy loads—attempting to do so would take the weight off the front wheels.

According to Syl Melroe, by 7 a.m. the morning after Cyril got back from the Mobridge demonstration, Louis Keller was out in the Gwinner development shop, trying to figure out how to put an extra set of wheels on the Melroe Self-Propelled Loader.

Louis worked closely with Cliff Melroe and Melroe Manufacturing engineer Gordon Irwin, this time building a machine with four-wheel traction. The senior Melroe brother at the company was a talented engineer in his own right—one without formal training, his cousin Syl said.

"Cliff couldn't draw a circle with a compass, I don't think. But he probably has the best mechanical mind of anybody I

THE ART OF THE DEAL

The Melroe loader seemed like an easy sell on paper. But demonstrating its versatility would be vital in getting across just how many tasks the loader could do.

Sometimes even the demonstration didn't convince—but determination usually did. Syl Melroe recalled one sales trip that started with a hustle out the door.

"A farmer called from Dickinson, North Dakota, and wanted to see the machine work in his barn," he said. Going through town, Melroe arrived about an hour and a half early, and saw a sales barn where cattle had been purchased the day before and were being picked up.

"I stopped and offered to show it to the manager of the barn," he said. Wary of yet another farm implement that wouldn't work as promised or deliver on cost savings, one of the barn employees tossed Melroe out. "'It's guys like you that make people like me go

broke! The gate you came in is right there, would you mind leaving?'" Melroe recalled.

Deterred, Melroe went on to his planned sales call—which turned out to be a court of appeal. "I went out to the farmer and demonstrated to him. He said, 'You know who needs one of these? The sales barn in Dickinson.' I told him what had happened—and he told me, 'You take it back there. I'm the president of the board.'"

Melroe returned, and went through his demonstration—and won a convert. "I unloaded it, and cleaned that pen. He went out to dump the truck, and by the time he got back I had pushed it all together in the next pen, and in another minute I had him loaded again.

"Before I left, that same guy came back and said, 'Where's that brochure?'"

>> *Early on, the Melroe Company decided that movies would help the company demonstrate how its new loader could perform a variety of tasks. In these still photos taken during the filming of one such movie, inventor Cyril Keller cleans animal pens at the West Fargo, North Dakota, stockyards.*

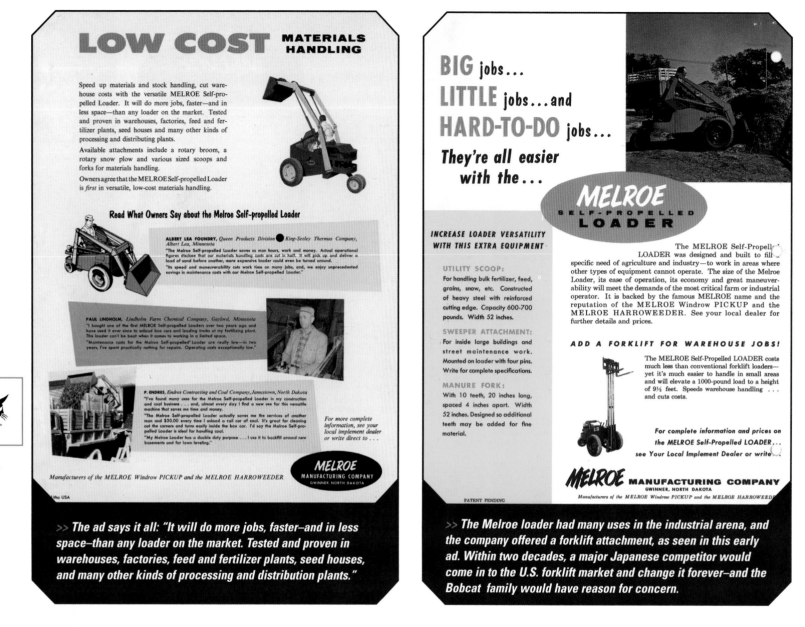

>> The ad says it all: "It will do more jobs, faster—and in less space—than any loader on the market. Tested and proven in warehouses, factories, feed and fertilizer plants, seed houses, and many other kinds of processing and distribution plants."

>> The Melroe loader had many uses in the industrial arena, and the company offered a forklift attachment, as seen in this early ad. Within two decades, a major Japanese competitor would come in to the U.S. forklift market and change it forever—and the Bobcat family would have reason for concern.

know. I've watched him do this many times: engineers will get done designing a piece of machinery, and Cliff will walk right up and say, 'Well, this piece should be a casting over here, and this one should be formed, and this one's not heavy enough, and this one should be done this way.' And he was right about 99 percent of the time. He would tell the engineers where it was going to break, and it did."

With help from Irwin in describing his ideas to trained engineers, Cliff and the Kellers set out to improve the loader with an extra set of wheels. Two of the key aspects of the four-wheeler's design were determining the proper weight balance and wheelbase. The team decided that a 70-30 weight ratio was best: when empty, the machine should have 70 percent of its weight on the back end, and 30 percent on the front. Fully laden, the ratios should be reversed for maximum maneuverability and traction. They also extended the M200's length by 6 inches, providing more stability while still allowing the loader to turn in its own tracks.

By the time those changes were made, the developers of the Melroe loader had in essence created the first skid-steer loader. Properly balanced, the loader would skid on its tires when turning—not enough to abrade the tires, but enough to

>> This M400, marketed under the Farmhand brand, was one of the first four-wheel skid-steer loaders to be built in 1960. Even though the M400 didn't set any sales records, it formed the mechanical blueprint for hundreds of thousands of skid-steer loaders to come.

make it easily maneuverable. That M400, with four-wheel-drive, wouldn't set any sales records, but it formed the mechanical blueprint for hundreds of thousands of skid-steer loaders to come—from the Melroe Company and other makers as well. For less than two thousand 1960 dollars, the Melroe loader would do the work of many men—a proposition an increasing number of customers found difficult to resist.

>> Louis Keller lifts and dumps loads of dirt on a construction site with a prototype of the M440. For less than $2,000, the Melroe loader would do the work of many men—a proposition an increasing number of customers found difficult to resist.

A ROUGH START

Even as the loader was gaining a reputation for usefulness, more technical challenges emerged. The four-wheel loaders had one problem in particular that nearly pushed the Melroe Company out of the loader business—the chain. Exposed to the elements, the chain constantly collected dirt as the loader traversed worksites that were dry and dusty one day and wet and sloppy the next. The resulting sludge eventually jammed the drive train and shut down the loader. Occasionally, the chain would just break due to excess wear and friction.

"It would frequently break down, and the service calls and warranty were killing us," recalled Syl Melroe.

"You'd run into one problem and solve it, and then you'd tackle the next problem," Irving Melroe later said of the new four-wheel machine. "We frequently talked about getting out of the loader business. In fact, it was decided to stop production on the loader."

The loader business nearly met its end one day in May of 1961, when Roger, Cliff, Les and Syl Melroe sat with salesmen and engineers to determine what could be done. At the end of the meeting, unconvinced that the problems could be solved, "Cliff made the decision: we're out of the loader business, we're not going to make any more of them, it's done," Syl Melroe explained.

But before the company put the decision into effect, cooler heads—and customers in need—prevailed. Shortly after the Melroes' decision to end production, Syl received a call from the owner of a fertilizer plant in Graceville, Minnesota. The plant had a loader that had broken down, and the owner was angry. "We'll send a guy out in the morning with a pickup truck and a check, and we'll give you your money back and take the machine back," Syl Melroe offered.

"No, I gotta have it! Get the parts out here!" the plant owner demanded.

It wasn't the first time something like that had happened. So rather than stop loader production, the Melroes reversed themselves and set about finding a way to protect the drive chains—and to protect their newborn machine.

It was Les Melroe who came up with the idea of using a technique employed on old Case Model L tractors—putting the clutch and chains in an oil bath. The oil would keep the pieces lubricated, and enclosing the system would protect it from the dirt that destroyed the M400's drivetrain.

"We enclosed the drive system in an oil bath and that's when the loader took off," Syl Melroe said. "We could have just said, 'the skid-steer principle doesn't work,' and quit. That's how close the line is between success and failure."

DEMONSTRATING ITS WORTH

The new four-wheel loaders arrived at a lean time in the company's history. Sales totaled about $1 million in 1960—far more than any year the Melroe Company had previously experienced, since the harroweeders and windrow pickups sold for $200 to $300—but the sales force only totaled three men. The company as a whole numbered only about 100 employees.

The Melroes initially distributed loaders through an outside company, called Farmhand, but soon set up their own distribution network in North Dakota, and neighboring Minnesota and South Dakota. As the loader product grew more capable and more durable, the company needed to do more

PRICE LIST
FOR
MELROE SELF-PROPELLED LOADER

MODEL M-200 & M-400

		Weight	List Price
Self-Propelled Loader --------------- 2-Wheel Drive ------------		1600# --------	$ 1790.00
Self-Propelled Loader --------------- 4-Wheel Drive ------------		1890# --------	1990.00

Above units equipped with 12.9 H.P. ONAN Air Cooled Engine. 12 volt electrical system, starter, generator, battery, complete live hydraulic system, variable speed drive, and differential type steering.

ATTACHMENTS

UTILITY SCOOPS:	WIDTH	HEIGHT	DEPTH	CAPACITY	WEIGHT	LIST PRICE
	36"	18-1/2"	21"	4.8 cu. ft.	90#	$ 54.00
	52"	16-1/2"	17"	4.9 cu. ft.	120#	60.00
	52"	18-1/2"	21"	6.8 cu. ft.	130#	64.50
	52"	22"	24-1/2"	8.5 cu. ft.	145#	72.50
	66"	24-1/2"	26-1/2"	12.4 cu. ft.	205#	82.00
MANURE FORK: 10 - 7/8" Dia. teeth for 5" spacing -----------	52"	18"	23"		140#	72.00
9 - extra teeth for 2-1/2" spacing ----------	--	--	--		36#	24.75
Gravel Plate for Fork	52"	--	26"		66#	21.00
SWEEPER: Angle Broom	60"	24"			360#	575.00
ROTARY SNOW PLOW:	52"					695.00
VERTICAL FORK LIFT:	Prices and Specifications available upon request					

ACCESSORIES
Equipment listed below is optional and can be ordered with any machine.

Mechanical Brakes --- $	60.00
Chain Guard for 2-Wheel Drive ---	31.50
Motor Cover ---	29.00
Spark Arrestor --	40.00
"Led" Ballast for Driver Wheels --------------- 200# each ----------------	50.00 pr.
Cast wheel weights ---------------------------- 100# each ----------------	36.00 pr
Counter Balance Right and Left Side ----------- 42# each ----------------	8.00 ea
Battery, 12 volt --	27.55
Tube 7:60 x 15 (with Led Ballast Valve) --------------------------------	12.95

* Priced F.O.B. Gwinner, North Dakota
* Prices subject to change without notice
This price list supersedes all others on the Melroe Self-Propelled Loader
JANUARY 1961

to get the word about the skid-steer loader out to farmers, landscapers, construction workers, and plant operators.

What was the best way to sell the idea that the loader would make money for its users? Demonstrate the loader's power, maneuverability, and versatility by showing potential customers firsthand how to use it. Early on, the Melroes and Cyril Keller would look for work crews using men and wheelbarrows—then promise the foreman they could use the loader to do the work of three or four men.

Compared to most of the machinery these crews and farm equipment dealers were used to seeing, the loader seemed small. Some dealers were outright dismissive. "It's a cute little machine, but I have no use for it. My kid's sandbox isn't quite big enough," Cyril Keller recalled one of them saying.

The trick, Keller explained, was to get them on the seat of the loader. "I'd get on there, start it up, and the bucket would come up. He'd come back and just look, and say, 'I want to see it work in this dirt.' They had no idea of it because the concept was so new."

Keller and other Melroe employees logged countless hours getting the product into the hands of potential customers—traveling all night, if necessary, to get to the next stop on their list. Whether performed in a foundry, a fertilizer plant, or a container ship full of sardines, demonstrations of the loader's capabilities usually put to rest any notions it wasn't large enough, powerful enough, or versatile enough.

Unloading trains was one of the loader's strong points that took firsthand observation to understand. The loader's capacity of 1,000 pounds was at least 500 pounds less than larger equipment used at the time to unload boxcars. But with its turning agility, the Melroe loader would outperform those other machines, particularly the rear-steered models from Hough Equipment Company. No matter what the Melroe representatives encountered, they usually knew they could outperform the competition—but often they had to prove it.

One memorable showdown took place in Sugar City, Texas. Cyril Keller had to prove that the Melroe loader was the superior tool for unloading boxcars of brown sugar. The foreman set up a test—two loaded boxcars. Cyril and the Melroe loader would unload one while the refinery's own operator and equipment unloaded the other. Keller's boxcar had to be unloaded in one hour. If he missed it by five minutes, the plant lost money—the equivalent of the cost of the Melroe loader, so carefully were the sugar deliveries timed.

"I knew I could beat them," Keller recalled. "'I'll unload it just as fast as they will,' I thought."

Keller's intimate knowledge of the loader's mechanicals gave him the confidence to make the gamble. The machine that the facility was using to unload cars at the time had a shuttle clutch that spun its wheels as it left the car to dump its sugar. In the long run, that would lead to transmission problems, whereas the Melroe loader's very design anticipated such back-and-forth motion. Still, Keller recalled, "I was really uptight. 'I hope I can do this,' I thought."

"They got their best operator and away we went. I went right across the car, scoop and turn, scoop and turn. I was doing it fast enough that sugar would fly just from centrifugal force," Keller said. The other operator was performing as usual—and soon, Keller knew he was depositing three loads

of sugar to the other operator's one, or one every 10 seconds. In 45 minutes, Keller had cleaned and scraped out the boxcar—while the other operator was still working. Even without factoring in the cost of the transmission work that would no doubt be required on the other machine, Keller proved the Melroe loader to be the better solution.

>> *The earliest Bobcat skid-steer loader sported four-wheel drive for superior traction–and that opened a world of new uses for the loader, originally designed for lighter agricultural work.*

>> *The Bobcat loader made easy work of lifting and loading heavy payloads–work that would otherwise require three or four men for a day's labor.*

While agility was one selling point, the loader's size won it other enthusiasts. Keller recalled a trip to the docks of Nova Scotia, where shiploads of soda ash—used for making paper products a crisp white—arrived for unloading. The ships had large, egg-shaped holds in their centers, with 10-foot ledges staggered up the side to strengthen the ship's hull. The common practice was to send men with shovels into the ship, pushing the soda ash left on the 10-foot ledges into the central well, while a clamshell scooped out the load.

Keller put the Melroe loader into action. After bridge planks were laid across the central well, he drove the loader around the 10-foot ledge, scooping out the excess soda ash and dumping it into the well, keeping up with the clamshell. "That's where the skid-steer loader really proved out and really saved money," he recalled.

It took most of the next decade to firmly implant the notion of the skid-steer loader's usefulness, Keller said, but it grew simpler with every demonstration. "You had to get it off the truck," he explained. "Once it got out, people started to talk about it."

HOW THE BOBCAT BRAND WAS BORN

With the skid-steer concept fully realized, and a growing number of customers finding myriad uses for the machine, the company sought to build on its unique character. With a new name, a new logo, and a new paint scheme, the Melroe loader assumed a new identity—one that would become an icon of American progress.

It owes that identity to a single day's meeting with Melroe Manufacturing's new Minneapolis advertising agency. The Melroes had been looking for a catchier name than the Melroe Self-Propelled Loader. They wanted something that would convey the capabilities of a skid-steer—and would give the public something easy to remember. Syl Melroe, then the advertising manager for the Melroe Company, went to Minneapolis to create a new brochure for the loader. By the time he returned to Gwinner, the loader had a new color, a new badge, and a new tagline—and a brand-new name that would one day replace the Melroe brand name itself.

Syl Melroe arrived at about nine o'clock in the morning to Lynn Bickett's office at Gould, Brown & Bickett, the ad agency that had recently been commissioned to develop the brochure. Bickett, Syl Melroe recalled, began questioning him about how the machine was to be positioned. From fertilizer plants and dairy barns, two emerging markets for the loader, Bickett came up with a white paint scheme. "When I said the dairy thing I think white popped into his mind as clean and sterile," Melroe said. "So, that's how the white color came about. I mean this is like an hour after we started talking about this thing."

>> The body of a Bobcat machine began as steel and parts—and earned the Melroe badge after careful examinations for quality. Here the oval Melroe badge is applied to a machine on the assembly line in 1970.
Pictured: *George Wyckoff*

>> The Melroe Bobcat logo was created during a one-day meeting between Syl Melroe and Minneapolis ad agency, Gould, Brown & Bickett.

Then Bickett and Melroe began discussing the loader's name. The unique machine needed an equally unique name, and the Melroe brothers had been kicking around ideas of their own. "I think Bobcat had been put on somebody's list someplace, but it was one of those things that didn't stick," Syl Melroe said. "Irv had that list. I saw it laying on his desk one day. I didn't pay that close attention to it, but I'm sure there were other animal names."

Bickett and Melroe called for a dictionary from his secretary's office and started looking up animal names—lion, tiger, cougar, panther, and finally, bobcat. The definition in that particular dictionary described the bobcat as "tough, quick, and agile."

"Nowadays, when you look up 'bobcat' it's a 'North American animal, 18 inches high and weighs 40 pounds' and whatever. Well, that doesn't make a very good slogan, you know?" Melroe said. "But the tough, quick, and agile thing— bingo, that was it."

The final step was a new logo. At about 11:30 a.m., Melroe says, Bickett called in art director Ralph Ladine, and explained that the machine would be painted white and would be called "Bobcat"—and asked Ladine to work on ideas for a logo. "Lynn and I went out to lunch and came back at quarter to one, and Ralph had the logo done. That was the original logo, with the springing bobcat and Melroe.

"So that's what happened on one morning—we painted it white, and called it a Bobcat and made a logo all in about three hours, four hours. That's probably a pretty productive day by today's standards," he laughed.

OUT OF THE BARN, INTO THE LIMELIGHT

By the time the Melroe Bobcat M440 skid-steer loader emerged, late in 1962, the Melroe Manufacturing Company had already progressed far from its farming roots. E. G. Melroe's harroweeder and windrow pickup were still important parts of the company's business, but the new skid-steer loader's potential quickly moved beyond the farm-implement business.

By 1962, the Melroes had a considerable investment in the challenge Eddie Velo had brought to the Kellers. Four years

of development, a few false starts, a near-death experience for the skid-steer loader itself, and $350,000 in capital finally resulted in the Bobcat skid-steer loader, a product that would become a household name within 10 years.

The machine had matured from its three-wheel (well, two wheels and a caster), pulley-driven roots into a durable machine that was tough, quick and agile—true to its name. Powered by a 15.5-horsepower engine, the Bobcat loader had a lift capacity of 1,100 pounds, while remaining faithful to the initial concept of two steering levers operating a variable-speed, clutch-drive system.

And the company had matured to the point that it was ready for the spectacular growth that would come throughout the next decade. A newspaper account in 1963 reported on the growth of the company, spurred by the skid-steer loader:

With sales topping $6 million last year, Melroe Manufacturing Company seems to have moved from the realm of small business to the arena of big business. In

North Dakota, Melroe products accounted for nearly 8 percent of the state's total manufacturing income.

The "hot" item in last year's Melroe sales picture was the Bobcat, a small tractor-loader that is finding new applications almost every day in both farming and industry. In two short years, the Bobcat has boosted Melroe from a regional agricultural manufacturer to a national industrial manufacturer, with a nationwide sales organization.

The little Bobcat tractor got its start in 1957 as a handy machine for cleaning out turkey barns. Six years and several hundred improvements later, the Bobcat is at work in every state, in Canada, England, Australia, and South Africa, and the demand keeps growing.

Those first Bobcats were three-wheelers with a hydraulically operated bucket in front. Today's four-wheeler is a bigger, faster, huskier machine that still turns on a dime. In addition to handling a dozen different

MODELS

M60 1958   **M200** 1959   **M400** 1960   **M440** 1962

kinds of buckets, the present Bobcat digs trenches and postholes, tamps earth, drives posts, shovels snow, sweeps streets, and parking lots.

Bobcats are at work in underground mines, in the holds of ships, on rooftops, in hundreds of fertilizer plants and on all kinds of construction projects....

From a four-man staff in 1950, the Melroe payroll has grown to just under 200 employees this winter.

The Bobcat skid-steer loader would transform the Melroe Company from a regional, agriculture-based company to a far-flung international concern.

And it all sprang from the minds of the Keller brothers, aided by the Melroes.

"Today, how many million people make a living off that Bobcat machine?" Cyril Keller observed. "Off just one idea my brother and I had?"

TIMELINE

1947
The Melroe Manufacturing Company is in business. E. G. Melroe, 1892-1955, sets up the company in Gwinner, North Dakota, to build windrow pickups.

1957
Turkey farmer Eddie Velo inspires brothers Cyril and Louis Keller to design the three-wheel loader. The Kellers build the first prototype in their shop in Rothsay, Minnesota. Melroe's annual sales rose above $1 million for the first time.

1958
The Keller loader goes on display at the Minnesota State Fair, and its popularity leads to the Melroe Manufacturing Company purchasing manufacturing rights. The Keller brothers go to work for the Melroe brothers.

1959
The Melroe Self-Propelled Loader, or the M200, goes into production, with a 12.9-horsepower engine and a rear caster wheel for steering.

1960
Melroe turns the M200 into a four-wheel loader to improve stability. The M400 becomes the world's first skid-steer loader.

1961
Melroe nearly exits the skid-steer loader business—then improves its design instead. These improvements to durability ultimately resulted in the M440, released the following year.

1962
Melroe's executive and advertising team picks a new color for its machines—white—and chooses "Bobcat" from a long list of animal names. With a new logo, the machine begins to gain its iconic status.

>> By 1967 the Melroe Company was growing behind the strength of the Bobcat loader, but it still sold the products pioneered by E. G. Melroe—the harroweeder and the windrow pickup, as well as the moldboard plow. Pictured, clockwise from lower left: **Dale Webb, Dennis Mecklenburg, Bob Glas, Jerry Brown,** and **Don Lloyd.**

Bobcat
Comes of Age

By the early 1960s, the Melroe Bobcat loader had matured and evolved into a more powerful, more durable version of the loader Eddie Velo, and Cyril and Louis Keller, had first envisioned in 1956. With four-wheel drive, twin lever controls, a useful lift capacity of more than 1,000 pounds, and growing recognition in farming and on construction sites, the machine began to expand its reputation as the solution that got work done faster and easier.

"Isn't it interesting to note the wonderful way of life that we are enjoying today as compared with only a few years ago?" Cliff Melroe told an audience of North Dakota inventors as he presided over a period of unmatched growth at his company. "In our homes we can have almost anything we want by just pushing a button or turning a thermostat. On the farm or at our jobs, most all of the work is done by a machine that has been invented and developed by people such as you and I."

The Bobcat loader had already changed the Melroe Manufacturing Company, too—in little ways and in big ones—and throughout the decade, it would become the main driver of the company's growth. A mid-1960s account of the Melroe Company recounted how the company had expanded to incorporate dozens of new employees, not to mention the

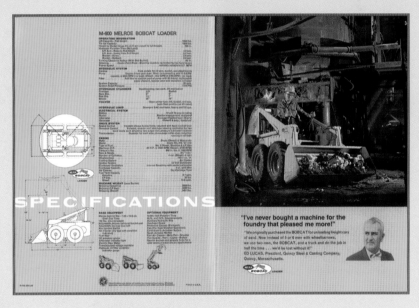

latest technology, to knit the Gwinner operation into a growing network of dealers:

President Cliff Melroe walked into his expanding engineering department office recently, scratched his head for a moment and commented:

"Man, I can remember just a few years ago when I would walk around the plant with all the dimension figures in my head. We just didn't have any engineers to draw blueprints."

The accounting department is talking about computers.

>> *The Melroe headquarters building at the Gwinner plant. By the end of the decade, new owners would control the company, but the name remained the same.*

>> *The Gwinner "International" Airport housed the airplanes that ferried Melroe personnel around the country on business. Here, a King Air poses with the Melroes' other pride and joy, an M610 Bobcat loader.*

And the sales office has a telephone that automatically rings dealers and sales managers all over the United States at the touch of a button.

The Melroe Company of this era was in transition—changing as the Bobcat loader took off, eventually to dominate the company's business. More engineers, more assembly workers, and more executives were needed. "The company was just growing continually," said Steve Jacobsen, one of the company's first demonstrators and a Bobcat dealer today.

To accommodate its rapidly expanding customer base, the Melroe Company likewise had to grow. Sales topped $6 million in 1964, and the company added eight new buildings to its Gwinner facilities by 1968. Yet, despite its bounding success, the company managed to hang on to its grassroots, family-run fundamentals. A local newspaper noted at the time that unlike their counterparts in major manufacturing hubs like Detroit or Chicago, the Melroes couldn't invite you to lunch at the Athletic Club when you came to town. They would, however, take you to Kay's Cafe, the oldest eating place in "downtown" Gwinner, for lunch and a piece of

GWINNER "INTERNATIONAL" AIRPORT

Visitors to the Melroe Company inevitably were surprised by what the company affectionately called the "Gwinner International Airport."

With a 5000-foot runway, the airstrip set up across town from the Melroe headquarters was an unusual facility for a company of Melroe's size. And while they were airplane pilots and enthusiasts, the Melroes saw the airstrip more as a necessity than as a luxury in the days when Gwinner served as the Melroe headquarters.

The airport linked Melroe with the outside world—including dealers and customers. Two airplanes were used—a twin-engine, 210 mile-per-hour Cessna 310 and a smaller single-engine Cessna 180—and approaches were made over a barley field.

With the airport right across town, the Melroes were able to service a wider area than they would have simply by car, given that Gwinner was a half-day's drive from Minneapolis. Along with the world-class telephone switchboards set up at the Melroe factory, the airport fueled Melroe's growth—and helped bring a little bit of Gwinner to the world.

>> *Gwinner "International" Airport had its own English taxi to ferry arrivals across town to Melroe headquarters.*
Pictured: *(unidentified), Cliff Horken, Bernie Doepker, and taxi driver Larry Schmidt (airport mechanic)*

homemade rhubarb pie. The only telephone at Kay's, the paper observed, was an extension phone from the Melroe plant.

RUN BY THE FAMILY

The family atmosphere at Melroe was fostered by the four brothers, their cousin, Syl Melroe, and their brother-in-law, Gene Dahl.

Dahl had married Evelyn (known as Evie), or, as he put it, "the best of the Melroes. The boys never argued with that." A Gwinner boy like the Melroes, Dahl knew the family "practically from the baptismal font." After serving in World War II at the Battle of the Bulge with the 75th Division—called the "Diaper" Division, since the average age was 21 years old—Dahl returned to Gwinner and joined the Melroe Manufacturing Company in 1950 as its purchasing agent, responsible by the time he left the company for about $9 million worth of iron, steel, and other materials each year.

As their closest business associate for much of the company's existence, Dahl recalled the Melroe brothers as uniquely suited for their roles at the company.

"Everyone was a baseball player," he said. "That interested them all except Les, and he probably wasn't as good a player as the others.

"Cliff I call an artist with iron. If there was something that needed to be designed, he did it—and he hadn't had one hour of engineering, it was just in his head. Also, from a business standpoint, he hadn't had an hour of business education, but he knew business. When it came around to business, he didn't give anything away."

Cliff, Dahl remembered, couldn't go into the service during the war because he had a heart problem—and hard work had made him the company president by the time the others returned. "Cliff was, of course, the president when the guys came back. He had worked his butt off during the war, because he didn't have a lot of things he needed because it was wartime. He was probably the strongest, physically, of the Melroes. I saw him use a two-handled scoop to shovel a truckload empty."

As for Les Melroe, he "doesn't get as much credit for the success of the company as he should get. He probably would have been president of the company if he hadn't gone to war. When you think of it, Les was the guy who was thinking out of the box," Dahl recalled. "He was the one that says we can make more than that—we can do this, we can do that. He had an office in Minneapolis and, of course, that was a little bit of a problem,

>> Following the death of E. G. Melroe in 1955, his sons and son-in-law took the reins at the Melroe Manufacturing Company. Seated are Clifford E. Melroe and Lester W. Melroe. Standing are Eugene R. Dahl, Irving L. Melroe, and Roger Melroe. "This is a rare photo," Gene Dahl says. "We were rarely all together at once."

having one of the brothers down there and three up in Gwinner. And when you really think about it, Les is the guy who brought the loader to the attention of the rest of us. He knew the dealer who was an uncle to the Kellers—Anton Christianson," he said.

"Roger was the most sophisticated of the Melroes," Dahl explained. "He was the consummate businessman. He always dressed impeccably. He didn't chase the ladies, but the ladies chased him. I don't think he got the worst of the race. He married Dorothea, and they had a wonderful life together. They fit.

"He was very successful in marketing. We sold 200 machines in one order to Monsanto, so Roger was very successful in that and in handling bank relations, two very important things."

As for the youngest brother, Irving, "He always kind of felt like he wasn't quite as up to speed with the other guys. He was successful at selling, but like the others, he went without any business education or training. He felt a little bit like he wasn't quite ready to go out and do this. But South Dakota was important for the windrow pickup—it helped make the company. And Irv was in charge of South Dakota and had a good effect on that."

"They were an unusual group, each with their special talents," added Jim Kertz, who started with the company in 1969

and retired in 1996 as the CEO. "They were a special blend; they went together. They had differences of opinion, but I never saw them argue."

If you were to see the brothers in a lineup—well, Kertz said, "a lineup might describe 'em. They were very innovative, hardworking, and I think I would describe them as risk-takers. They also had kind of a checks and balances among themselves.

"Roger was the marketing guy—and he was personable, go out and play with dealers, get them on your side type. And they loved him. It's pretty much the same for Irv, though he was more on the agricultural side of the business.

"Les was the innovator and the risk taker," Kertz continued. "He was always willing to take a gamble to finance an endeavor that maybe didn't look too good on the outside. I don't know how many ideas he looked at and tried to sell to the brothers.

"And Cliff was kind of the stabilizing influence on them all. He had a better feel for the financial picture because that was his responsibility. He would have to rein them in—not that he wasn't as fun-loving as the rest of them."

Of himself and his brothers, Cliff Melroe observed that their lack of higher education and formal training often worked to their

>> *As the Bobcat loader took off, the Melroe Company grew to accommodate production—as it had done earlier for the popular Melroe agricultural products. The plant was expanded eight times in two decades of growth.*

benefit. "None of us four brothers had the opportunity of getting an education beyond high school, so apparently we did not know what could not be done."

That philosophy worked well for the Melroe Company when its products were built on a smaller scale. But rapid acceptance of the Bobcat loader pushed the company to its limits—and even four brothers couldn't keep rein over the booming operations without some help.

Invention has a way of doing that, Cliff Melroe noted in a 1960s speech. "Usually a manufacturer of our size does not have the financial ability to involve themselves with more than one product. When I mention financial ability, I am not only covering the area of developing the product. Once the product has been developed, considerable money is invested in production,

maintaining adequate inventories, and financing accounts receivable, before this product results in a cash profit. It is because of this that many inventors are turned down when they take their inventions to a manufacturer. Many times the manufacturer already has more problems than he can handle."

The Melroes looked around them to find someone to run the daily operations of the business. They looked no further than the borders of North Dakota to find the man who would eventually push the Bobcat name to the fore—and would be instrumental in marrying the company off to a wealthy suitor.

MONEY IN THE BANK

Robert N. Spolum was the first non-Melroe to lead the Melroe Company—but Spolum was no stranger to the operation.

>> *Once a Bobcat demonstrator got the machine off the trailer, most dealers and customers were convinced of its worth. Here, a machine is shown off by a dealer, Brodie Industrial Trucks of Boston.*

Although a native of the relatively foreign South Dakota, Spolum had grown up in Minnesota and Iowa before joining the Gwinner-based company as a controller in 1963.

Spolum's mission was to make sure the company's speedy growth didn't spin out of financial control. When he was hired, Spolum recalled, it was still a relatively small company—worth $3 million or $4 million a year—and primarily oriented toward its windrow pickup and harroweeder machines. But the skid-steer loader was becoming a larger part of the Melroe business with each year.

"The Bobcat loader was not a very large part of the business," he recalled. "It was the one that really caught on rapidly, though—that's where the growth came from."

As it expanded, the Melroe's business often clashed with its books. Though the company had a clean reputation for finances, it didn't have access to the kind of capital that would allow it to expand as rapidly as it could have. Time-honored business processes and procedures—particularly, how to forecast yearly sales—had yet to be set up by the homegrown company. It all led to Spolum's hiring.

COMPACT BOBCAT LOADER

LIFTS 1000 POUNDS

Front-end loaders are one of the most versatile types of materials handling machines developed. They find use in practically every industrial application, including general manufacturing, construction projects, freight handling, mining, foundries and stockyards. They are as valuable to the farmer handling grain and fertilizer as they are to a municipality for snow removal and road repairs.

The Melroe Manufacturing Company of Gwinner, N.D. offers a four-wheel drive front-end loader which is extremely compact and maneuverable. The Bobcat Model M-440 has a 1000 pound capacity, yet can be carried in a pick-up truck. It will make a complete 360 degree turn within its own length, and can dump its load over the top of an 8 foot wall. The Bobcat frequently out-performs larger, more expensive units.

The key to the Bobcat's maneuverability is its unique drive system. It has no conventional gear box type transmission or differential. Steering is controlled by hand operated levers which are linked to four clutches, one for each wheel. Wheels on one side are completely independent from those on the other side. Pivoting is accomplished by reversing one set of wheels while the other set moves forward. Speed is infinitely variable from 0 to 7 mph, in either direction.

Originally offered solely as a bucket loader, various attachments have been developed to permit these machines to tackle many additional jobs. Accessories include: rotary snowplows, blades, pallet forks, grapples, back hoes, brooms and mowers.

The Bobcat required careful design in order to achieve high performance in such a compact machine. Torrington Drawn Cup Needle Bearings and Needle Thrust Bearings were used extensively in the drive mechanism to provide maximum load carrying capacities with minimum space requirements. Each of the four clutch assemblies contains four Needle Bearings which run directly on a hardened and ground shaft, and a Needle Thrust Bearing is located at each shaft end. Additional Needle Bearings are pressed into cluster sprockets on the lower jack shaft, and in the idler sprockets of the chain tighteners. In all, 32 Torrington bearings per machine have helped Bobcat attain its reputation as one of the best front-end loaders available.

Figure 1—Melroe Bobcat loader can dump 1000 pounds over an 8 foot wall.

Figure 2—Each clutch assembly uses four Torrington Drawn Cup Needle Bearings and a pair of Needle Thrust Bearings.

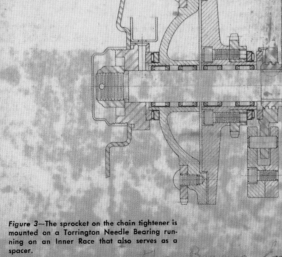

Figure 3—The sprocket on the chain tightener is mounted on a Torrington Needle Bearing running on an Inner Race that also serves as a spacer.

The Bearing Engineer

41

3

>> Bobcat films embraced the sassy, sexy '60s and the general trend to putting girls on machines whenever possible. Here, Jill Duis steps into a loader in the most attractive way possible during the filming of Bobcat Mania.

MELROE

MELROE BOBCAT
600

MELROE

43

"The Melroes were wild as far as spending money is concerned," Spolum said. "Once I got there, I started by making out an annual forecast. This had never been done by Melroe people. We had a forecast for $6 million gross for the year, about double what we had before. But the problem was, we needed a much greater line of credit" to be able to purchase and produce the machines needed to meet the forecast.

"We needed around $2.5 million in credit," Spolum said. So he went to the First National Bank of Chicago to try to extend the company's credit line. In an office on the higher floors of the bank's headquarters, Spolum beckoned the company's bankers to the window, where an old hotel was being demolished across the street—and three or four Bobcat loaders were knocking out the walls. "This excited the bankers," he said.

But the Melroe's reputation for spending—not lavishly, but quickly when it came to investing in new ideas—needed to be better controlled, and the bank invested its trust in Spolum. "The bank was very happy to see me come into the picture," he said.

>> *Like the car companies did with their ads and sales pitches, the Melroe company realized the value of pairing its machine with beautiful women. And by all accounts, many women were among those who took a chance on the new Bobcat loader and became expert operators in the process.*

February 6, 1964

LIFTS 1000 POUNDS 8′5″...
TURNS 360° IN ITS OWN TRACKS

SEE YOUR LOCAL
BOBCAT
DEALER

LANDSCAPING

CLOSE QUARTERS TURN

LOADING TRUCK

CARRYING BRICKS ON PALLET FORK

BACK FILL

HAULING SAND OR CEMENT

POWER...AND PLENTY OF IT...WITH THE **BOBCAT**

... Plus versatility and maneuverability. Four-wheel drive, controlled by left and right levers, operates left and right wheels independently of each other. Two foot pedals operate double-acting hydraulic system. Simple in construction, easy to operate, little or no maintenance.

- No Gears to Shift or Wear Out
- Variable Speed Direct Drive
- Compact . . . 54″ Wide x 60″ High x 80″ Long
- No Transmission . . . No Differential
- Clutches and Final Drive Permanently Lubricated and Sealed
- Positive 4-Wheel Drive
- Operates One Hour on Gallon of Gas
- Low Maintenance

...chments available include six bu... broom, pallet fork, back hoe, rotary snowplow, scarifier.

1. P. H. MACHINERY Company, Inc.
2023 West Superior Street
Duluth 6, Minnesota
Phone: (218) MA 4-5738

2. BARRON SUPPLY COMPANY, INC.
37 North Ninth Street
Barron, Wisconsin
Phone: (715) LE 7-3289

3. BAHL'S MOTOR & IMPLEMENT, INC.
Hastings, Minnesota
Phone: (612) GE-7-4164

4. GALVIN TRUCK & EQUIPMENT, INC.
Abbotsford, Wisconsin
Phone: (715) BL 6-2811

5. ARNESON & BENNETT EQUIPMENT SALES
Barneveld, Wisconsin
Phone: 2056
Branch: Hillsboro, Wisconsin

6. PAYNTER EQUIPMENT CORP.
1744 Cass Street
Green Bay, Wisconsin
Phone: (414) 437-7633

6. PAYNTER EQUIPMENT CORP.
4695 South 108th St.
Milwaukee, Wisconsin
Phone: (414) GA 5-5200

7. BROOKS INDUSTRIAL SALES, INC.
Sun Prairie, Wisconsin
Phone: (608) TE 7-5141

Manufactured by
MELROE MANUFACTURING COMPANY
Gwinner, North Dakota

MELROE **BOBCAT** ®

® Registered TM Melroe Manufacturing Co.

45

>> Design improvements made the early M444 Bobcat a success. Here, a model aimed at the dairy markets emerges from a dairy barn.

THE RIDDLE OF NUMBER ONE PLUMB STREET

The Melroe Company and Gwinner, North Dakota, had been inseparable since the 1940s when the U.S. Government decided to place its first order. And government regulations were the only reason that the Melroe Company acquired its first street address, #1 Plumb Street.

Bob Spolum recalled how the nonexistent address came to be an inside joke among Melroe employees and Gwinner natives. "A sales rep, Wally Shelley, had gone out and placed an order with the U.S. Government—the first time we had a multiple sale. The whole company went bananas," he said.

A month later, the government called Melroe and said they were sending an agent out to Gwinner to see the unit in operation. This was in the days when the streets of Gwinner were not paved, but were gravel, Spolum explained. "We go back in the office, and the fellow from the government starts filling out forms and asks for our address. Address? What address? He explains he can't complete the order without a proper address, and we say Gwinner doesn't have street addresses—it's just Melroe Manufacturing Company, Gwinner, North Dakota. So he asks us, can you make one up?

"And that's when Roger pipes up with #1 Plumb Street. We ask him, how'd you select that?

"'Well,' Roger said, 'You go a block east, west, north or south, and you're plumb out of town.'

"We'd get mail for years addressed to #1 Plumb Street," Spolum said.

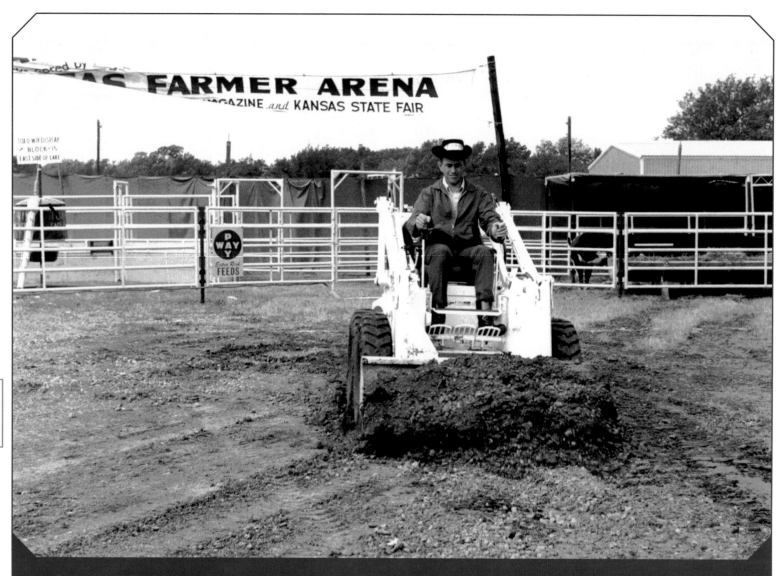

>> *Pushy, isn't it? The Bobcat loader made itself invaluable in all kinds of ways. Here, Dick Orr operates a machine for White Star Machinery, of Wichita, Kan.*

By the end of the meeting, the company got its line of credit. There were some strings attached: the bank required the brothers meet with its officers once a month to report on the company's progress. And then banker Bob McCullough took Bob Spolum aside to let him know an important detail he hadn't divulged to the Melroes.

"We figured you might have to have a little more," he said. "We have $3.5 million set aside—but don't tell the brothers."

"We didn't have to use it, but we became very responsible with the bank, and it gave us the ability to move forward and grow our business," Spolum recalled.

TOUGH ROW TO HOE

The company now prepared for building more skid-steer loaders—and, unwittingly, the challenge that a flexible, capable machine would bring. For every use the Melroes imagined for the loader, customers thought of 10 more. And inevitably, those new uses called for more power and more reliable operation.

The Melroe Manufacturing Company had made great strides with their machines' reliability. The M440 was substantially stronger and more durable than the machines before it. But successful manufacturing is a continual process of improvement,

>> *The race is on—by the end of the Sixties, Bobcat machines had retained the biggest slice of the skid-steer loader market, though they had competitors from America and abroad.*

and as Melroe engineers accommodated the needs of its users, they also set out to toughen the Bobcat loader's hide.

One of the simplest changes made at the factory fixed a problem with lug nuts coming loose on the wheels. Orval O'Neil, a Melroe engineer who led much of the machine's evolution through the 1960s, recalled in a 1980 interview that simply walking to the workstation where wheels were put on the machines made the problem obvious to a visiting dealer. "You got a guy on one side of the line that weighs 200 pounds, and you got a guy on the other side that weighs 140 and he isn't getting

them torqued tight enough. We got him a torque wrench, and that ended the problem," O'Neil said.

More liberally, there was a need to update and reinvent the machine for heavier-duty use. As the Bobcat M440 made its way down the assembly line, engineers planned for the M500 model, which was their response to the need for more power and the need for more reliability. The major upgrade was fitting a 24-horsepower Kohler engine, which warranted the change in model number.

Many changes to the machines involved running upgrades. "They were just gradual—one project, one change at a time,"

BOBCAT BOOT CAMP

If a picture is worth a thousand words, a Bobcat demonstration was worth a thousand pictures to the Melroe Company. Explaining what a Bobcat loader could do paled in comparison to showing dealers and customers what it could do—and thus, the Bobcat Boot Camp was born.

Boot Camps brought dealers to Gwinner—and later, San Antonio, Albany (GA), Phoenix, Tucson, and Fargo—to learn the ins and outs of Bobcat operation. Charged by the company to spread the word about the loader's abilities, the trainers—including the best trainer of all, loader inventor Cy Keller—taught salesmen how to show customers the value of owning a skid-steer machine.

Early on, Keller earned the nickname "Sarge," Bob Spolum recalled. "The new salesmen from dealerships would come in and spend a week there and he would really work their asses off." Spolum called himself a Boot Camp dropout—"although Cy liked to tell people he kicked me out," Spolum said. "I was not the world's greatest operator."

And while Keller taught the basics to salesmen—including lifting, dumping, turning the machine on a dime and scraping earth flat with the back of the bucket—occasionally the lessons would take hold a little too well. Keller recalled the story of the North Carolina dealer who sent a salesman, who was also a pilot, to Gwinner for Bobcat Boot Camp. After the week of lessons were finished, Keller took the pilot back to the airport—and watched him taxi and turn around several times without taking off.

"'I'm still running the loader and I'm scared to take off,' he said." The controls of the Bobcat machine worked in opposition to those on the plane, where foot pedals controlled steering. "He finally took off—but not without a lot of thinking," Keller chuckled.

O'Neil recalled. So far, the biggest change in the machine's history had been adding clutch chain lubrication on the M444. Over time, engineers would adapt machines to diesel engines; engineers were even charged with developing an electric version for grain facilities, leading to the M500E.

But a virtual rethink of the Bobcat loader was necessary for the machine to meet tougher and tougher customer expectations. Jim Bauer, hired as the Melroe Company's chief engineer in August, 1966, recalled that while the shape of the basic loader didn't change until 1972, the mechanicals changed much earlier, as Melroe adopted interchangeability to make its machines more reliable and more easily repaired.

"We had what I called the VW syndrome," Bauer said of late-1960s Bobcat skid-steer loaders. "Volkswagens had the same problem following World War II: they worked good when they worked, but they fell apart. So what VW did, they redesigned all the parts that were failing and made them stronger and better, but they kept them all interchangeable with all the cars they were building.

"So we did the same thing to the loaders. From 1966 until about 1969 we redesigned practically every part in the Bobcat powertrain, including the introduction of the Wisconsin air-cooled engine. [That] engine was installed so that the air was drawn in on the upper rear corner of the frame, away from the dust and dirt, so it would stay cool." Other adaptations—heat-treating sprockets and strengthening chains—contributed to toughening the machines. By 1968, Bauer said, "the time between major overhauls went from 300 hours to 1,000 hours, but all of the parts were still interchangeable. So if a guy had an old Bobcat loader out there and was having trouble with it, he could install new parts and go from 300 hours [maintenance interval] to 1,000 hours on his old machine."

"When we first came out with the Bobcat loader, we had enough problems with it that in two years of sales we would just break even," Gene Dahl said. "After that, we got those problems fixed and it started really selling. Because we had other farm equipment, the company survived.

"Not too many people expected this company to make it. We did it by treating the customer like he was king," Dahl added, pointing out that Bobcat dealers were considered some of Melroe Manufacturing's best customers. "We depended on the dealer to give good service to the farmer. We used to say we'd spend a thousand dollars to get a 10-cent part to a farmer, because the harvest was everything to him. It could break him if his windrow pickup broke down. Having the pickup gave us that perspective and keyed us up for doing the loader right. If we hadn't had that experience, Bobcat wouldn't be what it is."

NEW MARKETS, NEW IDEAS

The original Keller/Melroe loader grew from a turkey farmer's needs to remove manure from a barn. Yet as the Melroes studied the machine and the people interested in buying it, they realized that farmers might not be their biggest customers.

"It became apparent that there were markets for an industrial-type machine, and it was then that we basically made the decision to go industrial," Orval O'Neil observed. In that sense, the new Bobcat skid-steer loader was a distinct break from the original intent of the Keller/Melroe loader.

>> *The Bobcat loader could be outfitted with a vertical mast that turned it into the bricklayer's best friend. It could deliver pallets, and lift them during the construction of a wall—all without a single pulled muscle.*

"When we designed the Bobcat loader, we did not design a farm machine. We designed [it appreciating that] the real markets were industrial and figured that the farmer was not going to pay the money it would take to build this machine. We were trying to sell M200s and M400s for $1,700 and $1,900 and $2,200 and were having a hard time," O'Neil added. "I remember the first price on an M440 was $2,750, and we raised it quite soon. I recall Syl Melroe saying, 'Well, you can write off the farm market.'"

Selling the new machine proved difficult when the concept was new. "We went through a lot of times when we weren't selling enough," Syl recalled. "At one point Cliff sent us a picture

of Bobcat loaders sitting out there unsold on a lot, with a note to 'get rid of 'em.'" They had to make some tough sales to get things going.

But as the 1960s rolled on, word on the skid-steer loader began to spread, and new markets opened up to the machine— bringing with them new ideas on potential uses. As farm businesses turned their backs on the relatively expensive machine—a windrow pickup sold for a few hundred dollars, a Bobcat loader a few thousand—industry scooped up the new machine with the Bobcat logo. Fertilizer plants were one of the early adopters. Small blending plants were being built across the country as agriculture began to put together megafarms from

52

LEARNING THE LINGO

Since the Bobcat loader was a new kind of machine meant for doing new kinds of work, it grew its own language—starting from the phrase "skid-steer loader," so named because the lighter end's wheels (the front when empty, the rear when fully loaded) would skid around as the machine pivoted on its fronts. Folks who learned how to use the loader had to learn the lingo that came with the machine.

The reverse was true for the Bobcat sales force. In every new industry they entered, salesmen like Syl Melroe had to become instant experts on the business to be able to close a sale.

"Sometimes we learned more from the contractor we taught. It was a learning experience," Syl Melroe remembered. "Every day was a new day when you went out with a Bobcat loader."

That came down to the jargon that every industry has, Melroe added. "The cemetery business, for example, has its own words. One of our demonstrators went into a cemetery to show the workers 'how to dig graves.' The guy just about threw him out of the room. 'We don't dig graves, we make openings.' Don't tell a cemetery manager you dig graves."

When it came to mining, another language had to be learned. "In a mine, that's not the front—it's the face," Syl recalled. "That's not the ceiling, it's the back. You had to learn the jargon—and you better know what you're talking about."

"We were becoming experts in things we never imagined we would. You couldn't go to college and in a hundred years learn what you'd learn in a year of sales," he said.

Syl Melroe

53

The Melroe BOBCAT . . . Lovely little homewrecker

The Melroe BOBCAT Loader is a lot of fun to play with . . . but really serious about her work. Demolition contractors can hardly keep their hands off her. She can make a shambles out of a ground floor kitchen in seconds or go up 20 stories to wreck an entire bachelor pad in minutes. Barely 5 feet high and 54 inches across the hips, the M-600 can really maneuver in those hard-to-get-at places.

You wouldn't carry her across the threshold but the M-600 weighs a mere 3,269 lbs. . . . so hoist her to the roof or sneak her up on the elevator. Give her a big bucket or Ho-Ram attachment and the Melroe BOBCAT will take down walls and dump debris over the side in a hurry. And you could get attached to 19 other easy-on attachments. She's no pushover either . . . positive four-wheel drive gives sure traction on any surface.

Cut your hand labor costs in half — finish every demolition job ahead of schedule . . . and below your bid projections. Just for fun, call your local Melroe BOBCAT dealer for a FREE on-the-job demonstration. Or send us a love-letter direct.

MELROE BOBCAT
Loader

MELROE COMPANY
GWINNER, NORTH DAKOTA 58040

WSJ

Please send free illustrated literature and price list on the Melroe BOBCAT Loader . . . and details on Free demonstration.

Firm Name _____

Address _____

City _____

State _____ Zip _____

Sales and Service Centers throughout the United States and Canada

smaller family parcels—and those plants needed loaders to move their product around for transport.

One of the machines that already served this niche was the Hough Payloader, a two-wheel-drive machine that the more adept Bobcat loader ushered into extinction. The Hough machine needed more room to turn around than the skid-steer loader, and had traction problems besides.

The Bobcat loader's superiority in fertilizer plants gave it enough of a footprint to start making money. According to some estimates, about half of the earliest loaders were sold to the fertilizer industry. This one application not only kept the loader business going, it paid for developing new versions of the machine and for expanding the Gwinner production facility.

ON THE ROAD AGAIN

As the Melroe Company had learned, demonstrating the machine was the best way to get customers interested in a purchase. Though on a much larger scale, demonstrations still seemed to work quite well when the market shifted to heavy industry.

In nearby Minneapolis, Bobcat machines found many homes through impromptu demonstrations. "We put a machine on a pickup truck and started going around to construction sites, and found that we could very successfully sell the concept of the skid-steer loader in construction sites," Cliff Melroe said. The company's technique from then on would be to bring prospective construction companies to Minneapolis and show off the machines in use on major projects.

"One of the fun ones I had was unloading a boxcar [filled with talcum powder] out there in Portland, Oregon," Syl Melroe said. "This comes in [as] ore, so you get powder to 3-inch-minus shapes. So anyway I get into this place, the boxcar is sitting here; out the door you've got these stairs that go down to a conveyor. So I'm talking to this guy about this hopper, how big is this conveyor, what capacity, he said, 'Well you'll never get that loaded. You can't do that.'

"You get in there and the talcum powder gets really smooth and slick, you can just slide on it, it's like ice almost.

So it's really smooth and slippery, but at the same time you could get enough traction to do it.

"So I went in and out of this boxcar about half a dozen times and just going really slow, and move the speed up little by little, and pretty soon this hopper's full and it's heaped up. The guy says 'Stop!' and he ran downstairs. I thought well, the belt must have come off or the motor quit. He came back and he said, 'No, it's running fine; no one's ever filled that hopper before.' He couldn't believe it. And you know, I was running it not much over half speed."

So effective were the demonstrations that Melroe required its dealers to buy two machines if at all possible—one to demonstrate and the other to sell. The company also asked dealers to send a representative to the factory, to learn how to operate the machine. The company found that difficult—even in an era when $300 would cover expenses for a week—but worthwhile.

The Melroes asked of dealers what they went through themselves. The brothers and cousin Syl would spend days and weeks on the road, visiting potential customers and putting their loaders in the hands of new users, learning and observing from them while convincing them that the new machine was the way to make their work easier.

On more than one occasion, the work was entertaining. Syl Melroe, on a trip to Salt Lake City, ended up at a new Holiday Inn with a swimming pool—and around it were large piles of rocks, dirt and gravel. The landscaper on duty had tried to replicate the mountain landscape behind the pool, but a backbreaking half-day's work showed little result. Melroe got his loader off the truck and dispensed with the job in an hour, creating a 20-foot-long replica of the local stretch of the Wasatch Range.

More often, demonstrating the machine proved to be a filthy undertaking. On another occasion, Syl Melroe found himself at the Maytag factory outside of Des Moines, Iowa, in the foundry where washtubs were cast out of aluminum. "We couldn't get in there until after 10 o'clock at night. That's when they shake out the castings, and we had to clean up the floor. This floor is maybe 80 feet square, with all this black foundry sand all over it—and over in one corner they had this big hole where you shove it in.

"So I'm cleaning up this floor and just going around in there, it's just as slick as can be and I'm having a blast doing this thing. It's about one o'clock when I get out of there, I'm wearing a white shirt and a necktie. I just took them off and threw them in the garbage. You could wash that thing a hundred times and you wouldn't get it clean," Melroe laughed.

THE BOBCAT SQUARE DANCE

Of all the demonstrations performed at Melroe meetings, the Bobcat Square Dance is easily the most memorable, for employees and dealers as well as fans of TV's *Captain Kangaroo,* which used footage of the Square Dance when the Captain was shown on a farm.

The Dance, which started as a tip of the hat to Bobcat dealers, had been developed to show off the machine's skills for dealers, and was later filmed for a series made by the Melroe Company to promote the skid-steer loader. The idea came about because the machine's maneuverability, to some, seemed almost human.

The original Square Dance was written and planned out for a film entitled "Bobcat Is a Farm Boy at Heart." A handful of expert demonstrators— Ed Larson, Bob Lotzer, Royce Granlund, and Frank Fouquette—took the machines to Cliff Melroe's farm and through trial and error and a day's operation, came up with the 15 minutes of film needed. And from there, the Bobcat Square Dance became an instant part of the company's folklore, taught by one generation of employees to the next, and dusted off for parades, television spots and dealer meetings.

"My kids and our friends would say, 'They pay you to go out and square dance?'" said Roger Fischer, a former meeting planner and Square Dance instructor for the company. "When you did it in front of a crowd, when that music started, people would gather around."

It was definitely a great marketing tool— but it was also a "grand experience to watch people when you did the square dance," Fischer said. "We did it at the Puyallup fair in Washington, and I went out to teach the guys, who then did it for ten straight days, every hour on the hour. After two days, they didn't want to do it anymore—but it kept drawing a crowd."

Fischer's addition to the Square Dance was the caller's script, but the words weren't of much use to the machine operators. "You didn't hear the music, the caller, anything when you were running a machine," he said. "It's all timing—watching what others were doing."

So instead of teaching by cues and music, Fischer leaned on his other expertise—licensing Bobcat merchandise, including scale models—to teach new Square Dancers. "The best way I found to train people was to use the scale models, and to set up four glasses like they were barrels."

>> *This scene from filming the Bobcat Square Dance film shows Ed Larson, Bob Lotzer, Royce Granlund, and Frank Fouquette performing the Bobcat Square Dance on Cliff Melroe's farm.*

THE BOBCAT SQUARE DANCE SCRIPT

Ladies and gentlemen!

All of you know what the term "square dancing" means. Toe tapping music! Swing your partner! Promenade! Do-si do!

Well, today we're going to exchange whirling petticoats and stomping cowboy boots for a little different twist on square dancing. It's a square dance alright, but it's a "Bobcat Square Dance," performed by four rubber-tired loaders. If you know anything about skid-steer loaders, you know they can turn on a dime, maneuver through cow barns and cattle pens with ease, and load a manure spreader just about as quick as you can say "Bobcat."

It gives me great pleasure to present the "Bobcat Square Dance," sponsored by the Melroe Company, a North Dakota firm that manufactures Bobcat loaders and other products at its plants in Gwinner and Bismarck. In just a minute we'll introduce you to the drivers and get on with the show. But first let me tell you a little about this dance these folks are going to demonstrate.

The "Bobcat Square Dance" made its debut back in the mid-1960s. No one is sure whose idea it was, but it surfaced when the company scurried to find some form of novel entertainment for some visiting dignitaries. The dance went over so good that it became the subject of a Melroe film. And it caught the interest of Bobcat dealers across the North American continent. They began forming square dance groups to demonstrate the Bobcat loaders at fairs, trade shows and open houses.

The film version of the dance also caught the attention of some folks who produced the popular

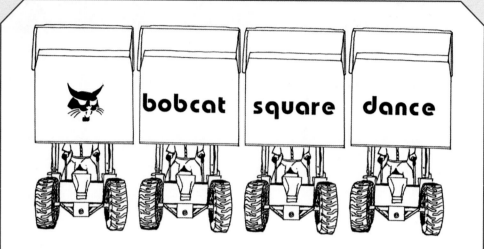

Dear Bobcat Dealer:

Here's an event that will draw attention to the Bobcat and your dealership this summer. It's the Bobcat Square Dance.....a lively routine that can be performed at fairs, rodeos, parades, open houses and other types of celebrations.

Yep, it's similar to the sequence at the beginning of the "Bobcat Is A Farm Boy at Heart" film. We've just changed a few of the patterns, and had them printed on the following pages. These step-by-step instructions tell how each of the four operators can complete the various patterns, and get back home again without running into his partner!

To get your Bobcat Square Dance team organized, simply select a couple gals and a couple guys (or four guys, or four gals) as your operators. Line up some bales or barrels in a vacant lot.....placing these props just far enough apart so the Bobcats can make their turns. Now start practicing. Timing and coordination are important to the success of the Bobcat Square Dance. With enough practice, your operators will be able to perform each pattern smoothly and with perfect coordination.

Once your team has mastered the routine, get yourself a record or cassette tape of some lively hoe-down music. Then, while your operators are performing, you can play the music and set the mood for the spectators to enjoy an entertaining square dance.....Bobcat style!

Best of luck, pardner!

"Captain Kangaroo" children's show. They used the film clip just about every time they featured the "Captain" in a farm setting.

I think you would be surprised at the wide variety of products and attachments that carry the "Bobcat" name. You owe it to yourself and your Bobcat dealers to stop by our booth, shake hands, kick some tires and see what Melroe and Bobcat is up to these days.

I've said enough. It's time to meet the square dancers and get on with the show!!

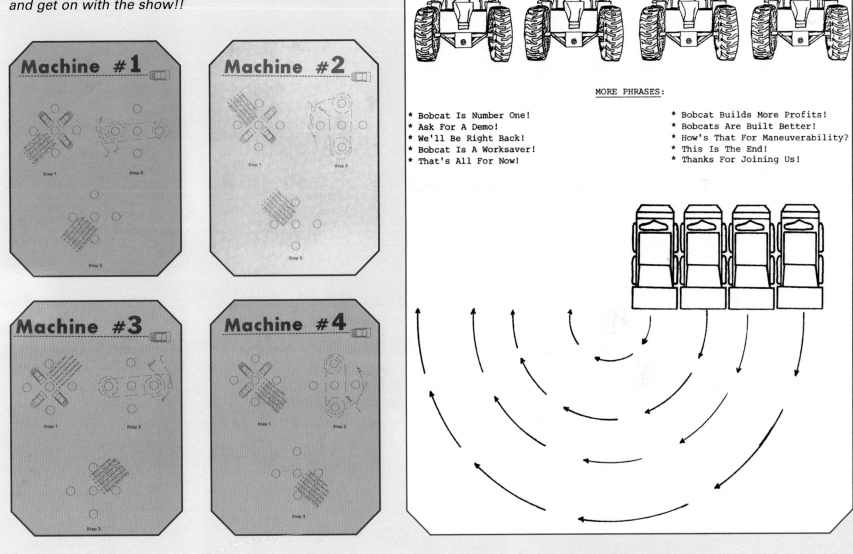

MORE PHRASES:

* Bobcat Is Number One!
* Ask For A Demo!
* We'll Be Right Back!
* Bobcat Is A Worksaver!
* That's All For Now!

* Bobcat Builds More Profits!
* Bobcats Are Built Better!
* How's That For Maneuverability?
* This Is The End!
* Thanks For Joining Us!

Machine #1
Step 1   Step 2   Step 3

Machine #2
Step 1   Step 2   Step 3

Machine #3
Step 1   Step 2   Step 3

Machine #4
Step 1   Step 2   Step 3

DEALERS BUILD THE BUSINESS

Demonstrations also helped build the burgeoning Melroe dealer network. When the company was strictly an agricultural maker, it was already well covered by a group of dealers familiar with the products, the needs, and the market. Selling the Bobcat loader meant convening a new group of dealers more familiar with industrial machinery.

Even with those dealers, an education process was necessary. Construction sales were stymied at first because of the typical means of selling heavy equipment—from an order

>> *A good Bobcat operator can get himself out of a deep hole with ease—thanks to the four-wheel traction and the Bobcat's perfect weight balance.*

>> *An M600 Bobcat loaders shows off the vertical mast option—a feature that made it optimal for use by masons, beekeepers, and fruit growers.*

>> Always one to capitalize on the trend of the day, Cyril Keller is snapped doing his Bobcat Twist with Squirt Waloch, secretary to Cliff Melroe.

>> Bobcat expanded its loader line with the M600 model in 1967. the M600 had a 1,000 pounds rated operating capacity. John Landby operates the machine outside the company's Gwinner factory.

Michigan. The company had been making forklifts and other industrial equipment, and had actually developed a skid-steer loader for sale under their Michigan brand. But that loader "just didn't work worth a damn," Spolum recalled.

Melroe executives invited Clark representatives out to North Dakota to tour their Gwinner plant and to hunt geese. And by the end of the visit, the Clark people were hooked. "They were highly interested in the product line and the market," Spolum said, "and they were very responsive to us."

At that point, the Melroe Company wasn't an overly large operation. While net earnings were much more, the net worth of the company was about $5 million—the aborted plans for going public pegged its value at $10 million. Spolum urged the brothers to consider an offer from Clark, and by his account, all but Les Melroe were very much in favor of a deal, and authorized Spolum to enter negotiations with Clark.

The meeting of the minds took place in Chicago's Prudential Building, where Clark had an office. The Melroes and Spolum arrived with their legal team from Minneapolis, while Clark chairman Walter Schirmer brought his own team of attorneys. Spolum would do the negotiating for Melroe Company, it had been agreed. And by the time the doors were closed on the meeting, "You could see 20 or 30 people in the room."

Clark Chairman Schirmer opened the talks with a simple question: "Cliff, what do you think your company's worth?"

The Melroe team had agreed prior to the meeting that a valuation of more than $20 million was appropriate, which translated into 500,000 shares of Clark stock. When Clark chairman Schirmer balked, Spolum carefully laid out the future plans at Melroe, showing how the line of Bobcat machines would be expanded to overtake the market.

Clark's initial offer of 250,000 shares left "a hell of a spread," Spolum recalled. Both sides retired to separate meeting rooms to discuss the deal, and, Spolum said, at the ring of a bell—like boxers in a match—returned for another round, "like we're going to fight."

73

>> Pictured are Bob Spolum, Cliff Melroe, Bert Phillips (Clark president), Jim Johnston and Roger Melroe on the day Spolum became president of Melroe Company in 1972.

Invention and Innovation

Clark's buyout may have changed the names on the executive offices, but it did little to change the Melroe culture within the company—and that suited Clark just fine. The Bobcat loader had been born out of ingenuity and pride in its North Dakota and farm heritage. Those traits—and an independent streak—would continue to lead the company through a period of unparalleled prosperity.

Simply put by Bobcat senior manufacturing project manager Al Michels, "We pride ourselves on being self-sufficient."

The company would enter a new era in the 1970s and early 1980s with new owners, but that wouldn't keep them from doing business the Bobcat way.

>> *Making hay: the Bobcat loader performed like a prizewinner in cattle barns. Here, Clint Lonbaken maneuvers a fully loaded M610. The M610, introduced in 1972, would remain in the company's lineup until 1982.*

STATE OF INDEPENDENCE

Clark Equipment Company had been formed over the course of the previous 65 years by mergers, acquisitions, and growth. The company's instinct for acquiring profitable businesses was keen—but none during this era would prove to be as consistently profitable as the Melroe Company and its Bobcat machines.

Skid-steer loaders were a natural fit with Clark's other industrial machinery. The company was a leader in forklifts, for example, and the lineup of Bobcat skid-steer loaders gave them a range of smaller-sized products that could be used inside industrial venues, while new versions of the Bobcat loader could be developed for other applications. Clark had seen the potential in skid-steers for a while before it acquired Melroe—in fact, according to Carman Lynnes, Clark had been developing its own loader in its Texas facilities for sale under its Michigan brand.

82

>> Cliff Melroe, Bert Phillips, and Roger Melroe (left to right) stand outside the Melroe Company offices. The company entered a new era in the 1970s and early 1980s, when it was bought by Clark Equipment Company. Luckily, the new owners didn't change the Melroe culture.

>> *Pictured above is a Kirschmann Spra-Coupe prior to it taking on the Melroe name.*

"The Michigan people took a stab at it and failed miserably relative to the cost structure of the product," Lynnes revealed. "Finally after a couple of tries, Clark said, 'if we're going to get in this business we're going to have to buy it.'"

And when Clark bought the Melroe Company, they had the foresight to leave the successful acquisition alone.

"Bert Phillips was the president of Clark Equipment Company," Jim Kertz recalled. "He had put out an edict among all Clark personnel to keep their hands off Melroe, to let Melroe run itself. It was one of the segments of the company doing well on its own, one of few acquisitions that eventually had great success. [Clark was] trying to acquire a bunch of companies to meld together."

Kertz, who retired in 1996 as president and CEO of Bobcat Company, happened to be the first Melroe person on the ground at Clark on the day of the merger. "I was in Michigan waiting for this to happen, gathering all this Clark material." Even then, Kertz dismissed any talk that Clark had simply purchased Melroe to shut them down or to move the company. "That never was even in the thought process anywhere," he said.

"The only changes Clark brought with it were in accounting procedures and also in the personnel area," he noted. "Beyond that, there was not a lot of Clark influence."

But the acquisition did mean the end of Melroe control of the company. Each of the brothers, save for Cliff, went on to other ventures. Cliff, Kertz says, "largely just went into retirement," while Les and Gene Dahl went on to buy the Steiger tractor business. Roger Melroe got involved with Bobcat and Clark dealerships out West, while Irv continued in the farm business in Gwinner and nearby Wahpeton, North Dakota. Kertz adds that each of the brothers got a good share of Clark stock, and became independently wealthy from the sale.

7:00 am   8:35 am   9:27 am

10:17 am   11:02 am   2:42 pm

4:10 pm   4:35 pm   6:19 pm

>> Bobcat loaders put in long days of work no matter what task was assigned. This advertisement from the 1980s captured it perfectly–from morning, to noon, to night, the machine's versatility paid off in work completed.

>> The acquisition by Clark Equipment gave Bobcat new venues for dealer and owner financing, as this ad made plain.

WE'VE GOT FAST, EASY, FLEXIBLE FINANCING

YOU'LL FIND IT WELL WORTH YOUR TIME...

...to let us show you the various ways we can help you put your Bobcat working for you, right now, with a minimal investment.

For starters, here are two basic plans, with several variations available to fit your personalized needs. All are backed up with the integrity, experience and resources of the Clark Equipment Credit Corporation.

RENTAL PURCHASE

If you haven't owned a skid-steer or articulated loader before, maybe you want to try one out for a while...especially the Number One machine in the industry...the Bobcat. Here's how: ● *Rent a Bobcat from us for a 3-6 month period, paying the normal rental rate* ● *Return it to us if it doesn't measure up to your needs (we'll bet you don't)* ● *Keep it and your contract converts automatically to a conditional sales agreement* ● *Rental payments will be applied to the purchase price, less interest.*

CONDITIONAL SALES CONTRACT

This is the most widely used finance plan, popular because it's designed to fit your personal requirements and payment abilities. It also offers you: ● *Competitive rates* ● *Variable down payments* ● *Easy monthly terms* ● *Physical loss and damage insurance* ● *Insurance financing* ● *Immediate ownership of equipment.*

YES, YOU CAN AFFORD A BOBCAT LOADER

bobcat®

CLARK

"I'm sure the decision was the right one because everything has turned out right," Dahl said. "The way the company has grown, Gwinner has grown, Bismarck has prospered—it had to be the right decision."

STATE OF THE ART

Right away, the Clark merger enabled the Melroe organization to spread its wings in some important ways. Dealers could always depend on support from Melroe, but Clark's deep pockets opened up a variety of financing options through Clark Equipment Credit Corporation for both dealers and customers.

Joining the Clark empire also gave Melroe the opportunity to begin to upgrade its facilities. Melroe was the significant employer in Gwinner, and with the business growing, finding more people to move to the town—or drive up to 90 miles each way, each day from Fargo—became more difficult. As the largest manufacturing employer in the state, Melroe had been wooing executives from other companies in other cities to come work on the prairie, but not always successfully.

Expanding out from Gwinner—a town of 623 people in 1970, which was a 150-percent boost from 1960—enabled Melroe to get more production capacity and to tap other markets for employees.

"Clark gave us the money we needed to expand, to grow with brick and mortar, to bring in the proper equipment we needed," Spolum explained. "We had the opportunity to go out and make acquisitions." Under Clark's first few years of tenure, Melroe purchased Bismarck-based manufacturer Kirschmann in 1973 for its Spra-Coupe crop sprayer, then inherited a former Clark plant in Spokane, Washington, in which it would produce Bobcat loaders for a short time.

"Over the years we expanded the Bobcat line through those abilities to grow—not only the business but manufacturing facilities and people," Spolum pointed out. "We could go out and buy opportunities."

And throughout the Clark era, the company would face the same technological challenges that all American industry confronted in the 1970s and 1980s. Computerization, robotization, and the arrival of serious competition from

BUILDING A SAFER SKID-STEER LOADER

While the first decade of the Bobcat loader was devoted to making the machine more capable and reliable, the second saw major technological advances in its safety.

Using a loader was itself a way of avoiding injury, Syl Melroe explained. "We developed the phrase, 'if it weighs over 50 pounds, go get the loader.' Don't let some guy hurt his back trying to pick up whatever it is. Just go do it with the machine."

But the focus on safety on the Bobcat loader, led to standard rollover-protective structures, seat belts, and seat bars, and new interlock technology.

Over the course of the decades, the Bobcat brand added the most standard safety equipment of all the skid-steer loader makers. Seatbelts and rollover-protective structures came first. In March of 1972, Bobcat installed an overhead guard as standard equipment on the already-on-the-market M610 and M700. The M970 and M371 were launched with overhead guards as standard equipment.

In 1973, the company decided to ship every machine from the factory with an overhead guard on it. Recalled chief engineer Jim Bauer, "We worked with the other manufacturers, and by 1974, every brand had overhead guards (ROPS, or rollover protective structures) and seat belts on their loaders."

The Bobcat seat bar was introduced in 1981 as a secondary restraint system and armrest.

"We struggled with what we were going to do," said Carman Lynnes, Bobcat engineer and one of the designers of the machine's seat bar. "But the company never stood in the way of doing the right thing," he says, even when it meant adding $300 in cost to the machine.

In the 1990s Bobcat developed and patented a complete lockup safety system—called BICS—for the machines.

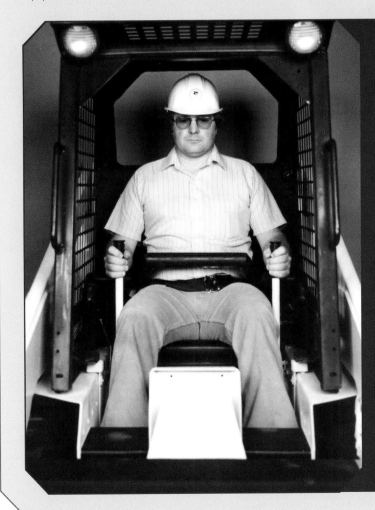

>> *Safety testing skid-steer loaders was taken to extremes, in the interest of protecting operators. To "field test" the new rollover protective structure (ROPS), this M610 was rolled down a hill at a gravel pit in Lisbon, North Dakota—and started right up after being rolled back upright.*

>> *Bobcat videographer Jim Moore demonstrates the Bobcat seat bar, which was introduced in 1981 as a secondary restraint system and armrest. "The company never stood in the way of doing the right thing, even when it meant adding $300 in cost to the machine," said Carman Lynnes, Bobcat engineer and one of the seat bar's designers.*

Asian machine makers would task the team with producing better machines less expensive—and the Clark organization would be a benefit in assisting Bobcat machines through that transition, too.

The Melroe Company had realized that technology and production would need a near-total makeover as the first years of Clark ownership unfolded. Melroe's production process had been "very, very manual," according to Grover Riebe, director of manufacturing technology at today's Bobcat Company. "There were no robotics, no computer-aided design (CAD) systems." Some body parts were pieced together in the Cooperstown plant, then transported to Gwinner for more handwork and assembly. Different assembly lines, new procedures, changes as small as a 10-cent rubber part and as large as the installation of a 400-ton-capacity sheetmetal press would be instituted under Clark as the Melroe Company transformed itself into today's leaner Bobcat Company.

>> *Throughout the 1980s, Bobcat engineers worked on making the machines stronger, more durable, and less expensive to produce. Here the main frame of a machine is welded together using a robotic welder.*

"It was a learning process for all of us," Riebe said. "That's what got us started down the road of continuous improvement. How could we do things better and how could we do it faster? The challenge at the time, because everything was manual, was capacity. How could we change things to meet the volume demands that our customers were looking for?"

It was clear the company was going to have to build its products faster and for less money. Over the next decade, the rise of the Bobcat brand would be threatened by competition that would make the company rethink the very way it did business.

RESPONDING TO THE MARKETPLACE

Clark's Melroe Division owed its speedy growth to its customers. It was an unpredictable business, with ups and downs based on the farming, housing and industrial economies. And it was always a challenge, employees repeat in unison, because customers were always finding new ways of using—and abusing—their machines.

>> *Clean-up is a Bobcat skid-steer loader's specialty. Whether on construction sites or in industrial applications, versatile Bobcat loaders spared workers long hours of physical labor.*

>> In 1969 Clark Equipment Company acquired the Melroe Company, yet the new owners allowed Bobcat greater autonomy than most would have predicted. Here, the Bobcat skid-steer loader and a Melroe grain drill take center stage in a circle of Clark products gathered for a board of directors meeting.

FARGO, HERE WE COME

When the Melroe brothers sold their namesake company to Clark Equipment Company in 1969, the company culture they created sustained itself in tiny Gwinner, North Dakota. As part of an international conglomerate, though, the company soon found that its business needs outstripped the area's infrastructure. So, in 1976, Clark decided with the Bobcat organization that a move was necessary—a move to the biggest city in North Dakota: Fargo.

Roger Fischer, former parts merchandising manager for Bobcat who had joined the company in 1974, observed that the move from Gwinner to Fargo brought Bobcat closer to the business world, while leaving a part of its Melroe history back in Gwinner.

"I think the fact that we were a family, one of the hardest things that we had to adjust to was moving from Gwinner to Fargo. For about a year we hung together because we were in a foreign country. We were used to being close together," he said. "We would hang out together for about a year and have beers together, then it kind of faded away."

"As time went on and the company got bigger, we all got busier," Jim Kertz agreed. "We didn't have the same kind of time available to us."

Of course, today's Bobcat also includes factories in Bismarck, France, the Czech Republic, and China. But a visit to the Gwinner plant today shows that a bit of the Melroe culture survives. Employees with the tenure to remember the Melroe days still speak fondly of the "family atmosphere" the brothers promoted. And if you happen to visit Marketing Services around lunch hour, you might come across a bridge game that once included Cliff Melroe's bids and plays—a bridge game that's been going on for over 40 years.

>> *In 1976, Clark Equipment Company, with the Bobcat organization, decided that a move to the biggest city in North Dakota—Fargo—was necessary. Pictured above is the Manchester Building, which was Bobcat Company headquarters from 1976 to 2000.*

To figure out how to build a better Bobcat skid-steer loader, engineers had to figure out how to break them. Ed Larson, a longtime Melroe employee who watched the company grow from its Gwinner roots, said his job was to make the product "very durable and very desirable. If the product wasn't durable and couldn't meet the needs, they wouldn't have bought it."

Larson and his Bobcat colleagues discovered that customers could find ingenious new methods of working with Bobcat loaders—and in the process find ingenious new ways to break them. Bucket attachments were used particularly hard. Larson recalls that many users would at first use the back seam of the bucket, instead of the bucket's front lip, for leveling dirt. The front lip was made of reinforced tempered steel and was designed to take just that sort of abuse. The bucket, on the other hand, was made of standard metal and its back seam would eventually fail when repeatedly asked to do things it was never intended to do. Education, and changes in product design, often cured that sort of problem.

Owners and dealers also were a constant source of ideas for new attachments for their machines. For an idea to pass muster, however, it would have to rise through the dealer organization first, then make its way through a prototype stage. For example, an idea for an attachment that

>> *The Mini Bob emerged at the same time Melroe built the M970 "Big Bob". In this photo, Cyril Keller drives a prototype M371 "Mini Bob" designed by his brother Louis, at the first Bobcat dealer meeting in Chandler , Arizona.*

marketplace pointed out the distinct niche the original Bobcat loader had carved—and the reluctance of customers to keep ordering larger machines when other Bobcat machines or other methods could do the work.

Chief engineer Jim Bauer recalled how he, engineers Gus Wallace and John Henline, and the draftsmen designed the "Big Bob" M970 in 1969. "I sat down with a blue checkerboard pad and conceived the designs and gave the design ideas to Gus and John, and they worked with the draftsmen. We had an internal sales meeting coming up and they wanted news on the Big Bob," he recalled. "So we made a 1/4-scale cardboard model, glued it together and put tires on it from the hardware store, and that's what we showed the guys in the sales meeting. It was introduced in

>> *Chief engineer Jim Bauer shows off a scale model of the "Big Bob" M970 to a group interested in seeing the company's next new product. The M970 was introduced in 1970 as the first hydrostatic skid-steer loader in the world.*

1970, and it was the first hydrostatic skid-steer loader in the world. It was a fantastic machine."

The M970 was a state-of-the-art device when it followed the Mini Bob into the light of day at the Arizona dealer show. While still a true skid-steer machine, the M970 was much larger than existing Bobcat loaders. It weighed nearly six tons and could lift up to 3,700 pounds, thanks to a large one-cubic-yard bucket, a choice of gas or diesel engines and the power of hydrostatic drive. It pioneered the use of a rollover protective structure, which became standard equipment on all Bobcat models that followed. And it was offered with a powerful backhoe attachment as well as a variety of buckets.

By all accounts, the Mini Bob and the M970 were greeted with enthusiasm. "It's the natural thing that people want it a little bigger and a little better," noted engineer Orval

O'Neil. But it was a recession year, and in retrospect, engineers and executives alike agreed that the M970 in particular was too big a step away from the original loader's core strengths. The M970 was a more expensive machine as well, and even with Clark-assisted financing, fewer customers were able to step up to the commitment. And finally, its gasoline engine proved less reliable than later diesel versions, and the marketplace did not find that acceptable.

The Mini Bob had also encountered dissent in the ranks, but the M970 had been a much bigger gamble. And while it was a failure by some measures, the M970 taught the company a valuable lesson—that not every great idea turns into a great product.

EXPANSION ABROAD

While new products were the order of the day at home, setting up more dealers became Clark's priority for the Bobcat brand around the world. In the 1960s, the company had stepped into the international market with an agreement with the U.K.'s Luff & Smith to produce and distribute the Melroe Company's products throughout Europe. Unfortunately, as Bob Spolum and the British banks saw it, the company was not creditworthy.

"They went belly up, and when they went belly up, we had put a huge amount of semi-manufactured machines over there," he recalled.

The insolvency at Luff & Smith would have been disastrous if the Melroe Company had not moved in immediately to recoup its machines and assets—and to set up its own operation in Southampton. "Our first, our own company entry into the international market," said Spolum.

Melroe operated out of England for many years until it consolidated its offices with existing Clark offices in Belgium. A mid-1960s deal with Italy's Beltrami was brought to an end when Clark decided there was enough potential in the Melroe division handling its own European affairs without any licensing deals.

It was Clark's assistance that aided the Bobcat brand's international expansion the most, Spolum said. Clark's existing infrastructure in Europe enabled Melroe to access new markets and to enter new countries. Germany and Scandinavia were early successes, while Italy and, particularly, France were more

>> *A Big Bob M970 skid-steer loader demo in Dallas in 1973 lifts a load of dirt using a backhoe attachment.*

that worked at home worked abroad as well. And while those European visits brought encounters with extraordinary people—Al Capone's driver, in one instance—they were not devoid of difficulty.

For one demonstration and dealer meeting, Jacobsen remembers arriving in southern Portugal to set up for a European dealer event—and being informed that none of the machines had arrived. After phone calls to the United States, Jacobsen flew north to the capital of Lisbon and went to the U.S. embassy, asking for help in getting the machines out of Customs since the event was six weeks away.

"They said, 'Sir, you haven't got a chance,'" he remembered.

So instead, Jacobsen turned to the Portuguese embassy, and pressed them for action. "'Do you realize how much money you're going to lose for your country?' I said. Well, it wasn't two days later that all the equipment came—but they wouldn't let us put it together." The problem was a complicated one, involving labor rules and the number of pieces that needed to be assembled. A quandary Jacobsen resolved

difficult markets to crack. "Europe turned into a hell of a good business, but it was tough to break into initially," Spolum added.

Fred Hein, who managed the Melroe division's European operations in the late 1970s, recalls that being an American product brought its own baggage to the European market. "It was an American product, when American products didn't have a good reputation," he observed. The European customers were "very nationalistic by country," he recalled.

"It took a long time to gain acceptance in the marketplace. The Germans wanted German, the French wanted to buy French. You had to overcome that with quality. All the competitors were there in some form or another, at least a handful of European competitors. None of them came, in my unbiased view," he said with a grin, "close to the quality the Bobcat brand had, to its durability, its performance, or its resale value."

In many ways, though, the European operations paralleled those at home. As Steve Jacobsen recalled, the demonstrations

with a long, late dinner, and many drinks served to a Portuguese interpreter.

Finally, all the displays and machines were set up, and the event was a success. Jacobsen had even set up a big soccer match, with players driving Bobcat loaders and "kicking" a large inflatable soccer ball with their buckets. Mini Bobs were used as goaltenders. The event was measured a resounding success—right up until Jacobsen's team received a phone call informing them there would be a revolution in Portugal in two days and they had to leave immediately.

Other European events went off with relatively less fuss, but transporting the machines continued to be a logistical and financial challenge. In one case, a Bobcat loader flew across the ocean as luggage. "Cliff Melroe took it to England as excess baggage once we drained the gas out of it and removed the battery," Jacobsen recalled. "It was cheaper to take it over that way."

THE BOB-TACH™
SYSTEM AND THE WORLD
OF ATTACHMENTS

When the Keller brothers invented the three-wheel loader, they engineered it for a very few specific purposes. Its light weight and tight turning radius meant barn work would be a snap—and choices of buckets and forks gave the machine some versatility.

Fast-forward 20 years, to the mid-1970s, and the Bobcat loader is performing any number of tasks never envisioned, never even conceived of, by the Kellers. From broom sweepers to apple pickers to snowblowers to mowers, the little loader's versatility was amplified a hundredfold by attachments.

The earliest attachments—buckets and forks—were manually fitted to the loaders, a sometimes arduous process but one that gave a single machine multiple uses. Some were produced by the Melroe Company itself; others that worked with the loader were allowed to wear "allied approved" badges, indicating that Melroe endorsed their use.

"The first Bobcat machine was delivered to a fertilizer plant in Britton, South Dakota, in January 1961, and then you know it started from there," recalls Syl Melroe. "We had this straight bucket on it. We knew we needed to have a manure fork on it because everybody wanted it. I think the manure fork was the second attachment. In winter we needed a bigger bucket for snow, so we made a wider bucket for snow and used it for fertilizer. Sometime after that we found out that you couldn't tip it far back enough to get a load, so we made a new fertilizer bucket with a break in it, so it would roll back more and you could get more capacity in the bucket."

As more attachments were invented, the need to quickly mount them to and detach them from the front of the machine became obvious. Finding an easy way to switch between attachments became the holy grail for Bobcat. While some forces inside the company wanted to standardize around a few distinct machines outfitted with buckets or forks, the majority saw the potential of an interchangeable setup that would let the end user choose whatever he considered to be the most useful configuration.

In the late 1960s, engineers under the lead of Jim Bauer began work on such a system. "The Bob-Tach was the single most important invention of my 26 patents. It revolutionized the skid-steer loader," Bauer explains.

"I did the drawings myself. A salesman came in with an idea that was being used on smaller Dumpsters, but it added 2 1/2 inches to the 'head-space', the distance between the front wheel and the bucket. We needed a design that left the bucket in exactly same place where it was in respect to the loader, so it wouldn't move the attachment forward. When we came out with the Bob-Tach, it was in exactly the same place without changing the head-space.

"The secret to the Bob-Tach design was the concept of triple-wedging design. Everybody else has a quick tach that used pins to mount their attachments, and as you use them they get loose and start to rattle. The more you use the Bob-Tach that I designed, the tighter it gets. That's important.

"The first wedge is where you stick the nose of the Bob-Tach under the lip on the top of the bucket. That's the number one wedge. The harder you push up, the tighter it gets. Then there's a slant on the bottom of the Bob-Tach and a slant on the bucket, and when you swing it in, that forces the Bob-Tach even tighter against the top wedge. That bottom wedge is number two.

"The Bob-Tach never touches the back of the bucket at the bottom, so no matter how hard you push on it, it always has freedom to get tighter. Then we put wedges down through the parts that mate there and put springs on them, so as you force the bottom in tighter and tighter, the wedges that are fastened to the lever would use up all the space. As soon as it has the opportunity to squeeze up, that wedge drops down even tighter. So the beauty of the Bob-Tach was that the harder you used it, the tighter it got. And you never have a sloppy, loose attachment on a Bobcat loader," Bauer says.

Prototypes were running by 1968, and by 1970, the Bob-Tach system was on the market. The Bob-Tach system endowed the machine with quick-change capability and interchangeability. With periodic updates, the principle remains the same. The system has been a Bobcat hallmark since its invention and standardization.

"Now the wonderful thing that has happened," Bauer says, "is that it became the SAE standard for all skid-steer loaders, and it's now the International Standards Organization (ISO) coupler design."

According to Paul Anderson, global product manager, the Bob-Tach system could exponentially increase the number of uses of a machine. "Bob-Tach allowed the customer to utilize more attachments, and at the same time utilize his machine more," he says. "In the past they would only use one. Now a guy could take three, four, five attachments with him and use them all. We certainly used that as a selling feature."

"The Bob-Tach is the best patent that Bobcat ever held," he adds. The wedging action of the design was technologically ideal. And since Bobcat held the patent on Bob-Tach from 1972 to 1989, it helped the company steer the attachments business—to the point that competitors adopted the Bob-Tach fundamentals in their own designs after the patent expired.

The Bob-Tach became a big factor in market share as well, Anderson says. "If you sold a machine and two or three attachments, it was a high switching cost to go to the competition," he points out.

Anderson explains that most of the very popular attachments now offered for the Bobcat skid-steer loader were invented or refined by operators and owners of machines. Hydraulic breakers, Rockhounds, and buckets have been strong sellers, and each was conceived or improved upon by owners using the machines in real life.

"In the late 70's and early 80's customers were trying to find replacements for hand held breakers using the skid-steer loader. The customers ran into problems adapting the available hydraulic breakers to Bobcat and other skid-steer loaders' auxiliary hydraulic systems because of cooling and back pressure. The first breaker that Bobcat offered, in 1985, that was able to overcome these issues was developed by HED Corp., a Washington company owned by Don Wohlwend, a North Dakota native. Don was able to adapt his breakers to work effectively on the Bobcat auxiliary circuit. He later sold his business to Stanley Hydraulic Tools, which supplied breakers to Bobcat Co. Eventually Bobcat worked with another Ingersoll Rand company, Montebert, to develop their own line of breakers which are offered today. This scenario is the normal life cycle of attachment development," says Anderson.

"Likewise, the Rockhound—a landscape rake that kicks rocks and debris into a bucket, had been invented by Gary Erholm, who came up with the idea and tried to convince Bobcat management of its worth. When at first he didn't succeed, Erholm built prototypes, got into a motor home, and went on a year-long tour of dealers, demonstrating his Rockhound until dealers petitioned Bobcat to sell it. Eventually Bobcat Company purchased the Rockhound patent and brought the manufacturing to our plant in Bismarck, North Dakota. "We were able to bring it in, and using modern methods of manufacturing, were able to build a lot of them easily, and we kept the cost down," Anderson says.

Some attachments grew to be such an important piece of the business that they drove some of the manufacturing changes Bobcat went through in the 1970s and 1980s. Buckets were among the first attachments developed by the Melroe Company—but as the skid-steer loader found its way into multiple industries, new buckets were developed. The bucket business grew so large the company developed a specialized robotic station that built them automatically, from raw material to final welding.

Other attachments, like the Feller-Buncher, would cut the tree, replacing a laborer with a chainsaw. It could cut multiple trees before laying them down in a "bunch". A skidder with a grapple could then grab the bunch and pull it to the landing where the trees were delimbed and loaded. The grapple skidder replaced a more labor-intensive cable skidder. The whole process was a labor-saving program.

Throughout the 1970s and 1980s, bigger machines enabled bigger attachments, ones that could perform the work of a larger machine. Planers were a classic example: full-size planing machines were big and wide, and could scrape down a highway one lane width at a time. The planer attachment, though, changed the dynamics of smaller jobs, as did attachments for other concrete jobs, such as concrete pumps, wheel saws, and the like. Bobcat owners could perform the duties of an expensive, single-purpose machine on an occasional basis—and owners could "bid less than the guy bringing in the big hardware," Anderson says.

The Bob-Tach system changed the industry, tilting it in Bobcat's favor. By creating a universal standard to which hundreds of devices could be attached, Bobcat had created something like today's USB port—determining the hard points and letting smaller companies invent new products on their own.

103

>> *The first Bob-Tach system was introduced to the market in 1970 on M600 and the M970.*

A WIDE WORLD OF WORK

FOR THE BOBCAT SKID-STEER LOADER

>> *This piece of literature titled "A Wide World of Work for the Bobcat Skid-Steer Loader" helped promote the Bobcat brand and the skid-steer loader's value and versatility in markets outside the United States. Clark Equipment Company's existing infrastructure in Europe enabled Melroe to access new markets and enter new countries.*

With operations already established in Europe, Australia, and even some coverage in the Middle East, the major black hole had been the Far East. Through the Clark merger, the Bobcat brand gained coverage there through a Japanese company, Toyo Umpanki, which manufactured construction equipment under the Michigan brand. Clark wanted its Melroe division to link up with Toyo Umpanki to build and distribute skid-steer loaders throughout Japan. The relationship proved to be worth more than just the sales generated in Japan and China.

"They were fun people to work with," Spolum said, "but they wanted to take your equipment and redesign it. They wanted to know what you've got, then they're going to put bells and whistles on it. They had to be different." To that end, Toyo Umpanki was restricted to sales in Japan and China; eventually the company made inroads in Taiwan as well.

But it was Toyo Umpanki's knowledge of a big competitor's designs on the skid-steer market that would prove most valuable—and would keep the Melroe division from learning the lesson Clark was about to learn in the forklift business.

WHO OWNS THE TECHNOLOGY
Although Melroe had the clear leadership in skid-steer loaders, a number of issues surrounding patents, licensing agreements, and technology meant the company didn't have a monopoly on the machine.

Through 1966, Melroe had the luxury of a 100-percent market share of skid-steer

>> *In 1977, Bobcat updated its image with a new lowercase "Bauhaus font" logo to accompany the Bobcat head symbol.*

loaders. But with the success of the machine came a range of "kopykats", as Bobcat people call them, that not only copied the skid-steer idea but copied—or even built their machines around—the Bobcat loader's unique clutch-drive system.

The first consequence to the company was in market share. While sales and profits rose, Melroe's share of the market sank from 100 percent to 36 percent in 1973. Between fallout in the segment and consolidation, the company's market share rose somewhat, and by the mid-1970s, stabilized at around 40 percent of the market—helped, perhaps, in part by advertising that stressed to customers, "don't buy the kopykat—buy the Bobcat."

Melroe had been aware of the problems that patents and licensing rights could cause since the earliest days of the company. But it was in the late 1960s when the first serious competitor, the Uniloader, underscored the looming problem: anyone could build a skid-steer loader, even though the Kellers and Melroe Company had pioneered it.

"In 1966 or 1967, we found out that a guy in Cedar Falls, Iowa, was making a machine in his garage," said Syl Melroe. "We knew a guy who worked in the building, and we got him to unlock the door, I looked at the machine, and hell,

they used our clutches! He just flat copied the machine—he bought the clutches, put his together, and changed maybe a couple of things."

Not everyone was convinced that the "kopykats" were a problem. With more companies selling the idea of the skid-steer loader, Syl pointed out, Melroe's sales actually increased. People thought, "It must be good, let's go back and buy the Bobcat model."

The thorniest problem in the Bobcat patent saga surrounded the royalty payments paid by Melroe to the inventors of the three-wheel loader, Louis and Cyril Keller. From the day the Melroes licensed the Keller designs and hired the brothers to refine the concept into the skid-steer loader, the brothers had received a per-unit royalty payment of $15. Other companies not part of the original deal infringed on their ideas and the Kellers sued—and won, four times. After the Clark acquisition, the Clark company raised issues related to the validity of the Kellers' patent. To save money, Clark's executives decided to suspend royalty payments to the Kellers.

"Clark took the position that we were no longer going to pay royalties because there was no patent," Spolum recalled.

THE BOBCAT FELLER BUNCHER

Skid-steer loaders could be adapted to perform a wide variety of tasks. But some product development paths led to dead ends.

Such was the case with the Feller Buncher, a novel product introduced by Melroe in 1970. Users of Bobcat loaders had been fitting their machines with an attachment that would clamp around a tree trunk, shear it off, and carry the tree vertically. The attachment, built by Morbark Industries, seemed to have wider application in the forestry industry, so the Melroe company took its new M970 chassis and developed a distinct 1074 Feller Buncher model.

Durability proved an issue with the initial machines. Engineers upgraded the drivetrain with heavier-duty planetary drives manufactured by Clark and called it the 1080 Feller Buncher.

But even the upgrades and a smaller, six-wheeled version, the 1213, couldn't make a sound business case. The unpredictable forestry business and the mechanical issues surrounding the machine compelled Melroe to sell the feller buncher business in 1987.

>> *Though the Bobcat product quickly became the focus of the company, Melroe continued to produce agricultural machinery until most of it was divested by the end of the 1980s.* Pictured: *Jack Wilson, an unidentified operator, and Bob Spolum with the short-lived Melroe cropmaster.*

The Kellers then sued Melroe and Clark. Because the Melroe Company still existed on paper—Clark had bought only the assets of the company—Clark took the position that it was not responsible for royalty payments. The suit wended its way through federal courts, and the case consumed hundreds of thousands of dollars in legal fees. Eventually, Clark authorized Bob Spolum to make a settlement offer—a "very substantial" offer, Spolum insisted—to the Kellers to settle the lawsuit. The Kellers turned down the settlement and eventually the courts ruled in their favor.

INNOVATION, INVENTION, AND THE NEW BREED

After the relative failure of the M970, the company refocused on the core Bobcat machines, and on making more profit from them. Business had been strong early in the decade leading up to the Clark acquisition, and by the year 1971, Melroe sales netted the Clark conglomerate $28.7 million—a substantial increase from Melroe's sales of $300,000 in 1950.

The growth at Melroe had come mostly from loader sales, with a smaller proportion due to the augmented lineup of agricultural products. The company had added the Spra-Coupe

>> *An ad for Bell helicopters featured the Bobcat loader.*

>> *A Bobcat M610 skid-steer loader with an angle broom attachment sweeps an area at the Gwinner airport. After the relative failure of the M970, the company refocused on its core Bobcat machines, like the M610.*

>> *Battlebots? No, just twin M970s loading snow during a hard Gwinner winter in 1975.*

THE PITFALLS OF GOING GLOBAL

It's unquestioned that Bobcat's move to go global in the 1960s and 1970s paid off handsomely for the company. But on occasion, it made life very, very interesting for the sales staff.

Fred Hein, who traveled overseas for the company from 1973 to 1977, recalled several trade missions behind the old Iron Curtain, where even in the morning, "they were drinking strong. By the time we got done, one prospective customer was so drunk they had to take him out of there by hand," he said.

Some places proved too dangerous for business. During the 1970s, Argentina suffered through waves of violence and kidnappings, and Americans were not safe crossing the country's borders.

And in other South American countries, safety wasn't a question—but the political connections of certain customers were. Bobcat's dealer in Caracas, Venezuela, earned the semi-affectionate handle of Commandante after Hein's visits to his country. "They'd pick me up in a big limousine," he recalled. "The guy I dealt with carried guns. He had a nice apartment house for his family, and each member had a floor to themselves. Five levels, three or four daughters, and a lower level full of new automobiles. When he came up here to visit, which was two or three times, he bought Rolex watches."

>> *Europe, Asia, Australia, even the Middle East—Bobcat's round-the-world expansion left no passport unstamped.*

crop sprayer to the Melroe line, and in 1973 acquired the chisel plow business of Gysler Manufacturing out of Fort Benton, Montana. The Bobcat loader's growth would eventually lead to divesting the agricultural products, but by the mid-1970s, the company's leadership realized their ventures into larger and smaller products—the M970 and the Mini Bob—had led them astray from the essential, successful formula.

It was back to the drawing boards, not only to reconnect with core customers seeking a new version of the hardy M610, but also to develop a slightly larger machine, a more gradual upgrade than the M970 had been. The new machines would need to be more functional, more economical to build and service, and would have to incorporate the hydrostatic drive pioneered in the M970.

The clutch-drive system common to Bobcat-branded loaders until then would not be found on the new machines. The system from the M610 had reached the zenith of its development, and to create a fully competitive loader that was up to current needs and standards, the clutches had to give way to hydrostatics. The new machines constituted the first complete redesign of the Bobcat skid-steer loader since its inception.

Chief engineer Jim Bauer recalled the early planning process for the new machines.

"One day, Jim Strand came over to engineering and said to me, 'Let's play keep 'em out.'"

"'What the heck is keep 'em out?' I asked."

"'Anybody with a shear, press brake, and a welder can build a loader,' he explained. 'Let's make it more difficult than that.' That was the germ of the design of the B-Series loader in 1975."

>> Bobcat took its products on "Road Shows" to demonstrate their skills to the people who mattered—customers and dealers. The Road Show was used in 1970 to introduce the M970 and M600 models. The same "Show Van" has made stops at sales meetings, sales training "Boot Camps" and other special events for nearly 40 years.

>> In 1970, customers and dealers at a Melroe Bobcat Road Show in Sioux City, Iowa, watch as M970 and M600 loaders and a variety of attachments are demonstrated. The Road Shows helped inform dealers and customers of new products and machine enhancements.

MODELS

M970	1970-1975	974	1975-1990	313	1978-1983	642	1981-1986
M371	1971-1977	975	1975-1990	632	1977-1981	643	1981-1992
M610	1972-1982	722	1976-1979	730	1978-1980	741	1981-1990
M700	1973-1976	520	1976-1977	731	1978-1981	742	1981-1990
825	1975-1982	533	1976-1981	732	1978-1981	743	1981-1990
M611	1975-1978	530	1977-1981	733	1980-1980	843	1981-1986
M620	1975-1976	630	1977-1981	540	1981-1986	440	1983-1985
720	1975-1979	631	1977-1981	543	1981-1993	443	1983-1993
721	1975-1979	310	1977-1983	641	1981-1990	743DS	1983-1990

>> *Bobcat machines found a niche in public-works projects, such as maintaining the Rainbow Dam on the Missouri River in neighboring Montana.*

>> *Orange you happy you bought the Bobcat? Pardon the pun, but this machine makes quick work of pushing orange peels in an Orlando plant in 1978.*

119

>> In 1999, Bobcat introduced the 864 compact track loader.

4

Let the Games Begin

Like the machines it built, Bobcat spent the 1980s and 1990s on the move. Competitors had moved in on the skid-steer loader concept, but despite the inroads from domestic competition, including titans John Deere, New Holland, and Case, Bobcat was still the largest maker of compact equipment products in the world.

But as was the case in the automotive industry, the compact equipment industry was about to face a challenge the likes of which it hadn't seen, with the formidable power of one of the world's manufacturing giants behind it.

In the 1980s, the hard work that the company's sales force had put into international markets began to pay off. Europe in particular was a strong point, but the brand was represented in Australia and Asia, too. It was in Asia that the Bobcat skid-steer loader drew Toyota's attention, then and still the largest Japanese automaker.

In the 1970s, Toyota entered the American auto market for good, building its first U.S. factory. By the 1980s, they had also entered the industrial machinery niche—one dominated, to that point, by Clark. Toyota took on the U.S. market with a forklift of its own design, and within a few years had decimated Clark's market share.

The forklift had been Clark's primary product, and the company's big profit machine. The company began building

>> *The Bobcat brand was translated into Chinese as the Far East market began to grow.*

121

the devices during Word War II, and captured the market. But Clark, by some analyses, had gotten too comfortable with its near-monopoly in forklifts. They designed their machines with parts that were not interchangeable with the competition, and had to be purchased from Clark. No outside companies made replacement parts.

When Toyota entered the forklift market, it adopted practices from the automotive industry—using, in fact, some automotive parts that were widely available and less expensive. They came out with a product comparable to the

Clark machine, but at a much lower price. Toyota invaded the U.S. forklift market and took over, teaching the American manufacturers a difficult lesson.

By the beginning of the 1980s, the Bobcat loader had effectively replaced the forklift as one of Clark's most profitable product lines. But reason for concern was voiced by the Melroe division's partner in Japan, Toyo Umpanki. The Japanese company, which was licensed to produce loaders for some Asian markets, discovered that Toyota was planning to enter the skid-steer market. With a lean production system, a reputation for reliable products, and a slight edge in exchange rates, Toyota could do to the Bobcat loader what it had done to the Clark forklift.

Yet the folks in Gwinner were anything but quitters. Instead of folding up their tents, the company wheeled about and challenged Toyota—and their own way of doing business—head on. They completely changed the way they thought about designing and building new machines. Unlike Detroit, they kept Toyota off their turf.

>> *Toyo Umpanki (TCM) manufactured several Bobcat loader models for the Japanese market.*

122

>> *Bobcat's international expansion led to a whole new world of tasks. Here, a Bobcat works alongside the famous canals in Venice, Italy.*

>> *Carman Lynnes spent many years as head of engineering at Bobcat, seeing the company through such production changes as using Kubota engines.*

Caterpillar had examples of both paradigms, in Lynnes' view. The company rang up $1 billion in sales in 1963, putting it near the automakers in terms of financial strength—and certainly in the top 200 companies in America. That company had turned its sights on larger and larger equipment, leaving behind a significant slice of the industrial market for smaller machines. So while the company's earnings were growing rapidly, it had lost its ability to innovate.

"Caterpillar would never put resources into something as goofy as a skid-steer loader," Lynnes said. "They were not trained to take those kinds of risks. They didn't understand that market niche anyway, didn't understand the substitution of labor in that kind of job."

That, in part, was what drew Lynnes back to the Melroe Company and the Dakotas. He recognized how Melroe was transforming itself by hiring folks with experience at larger companies. Until then, "most of the people at Bobcat had never worked at a large industrial company, and had no idea of the complexities," he said. The risk-taking Melroe had always been open to also had its appeal for Lynnes.

The skid-steer concept, though, did not strike him, at first, as a winner. Lynnes was "a little bit skeptical," he admitted, until "I took a product home and got comfortable with it, to see what it could do. I was concerned about tire wear, and it is a factor, but minuscule in the whole range of things." And

with his Caterpillar experience still fresh in his mind, he "kind of wondered what, really, was so industrial about the Bobcat line? Why do they refer to it as the industrial side of the Melroe lineup?"

In his career, Lynnes observed that the company had grown comfortable, to a degree, with the success it earned in the skid-steer market. "We were doing what we do, optimizing it instead of doing what the customer is saying."

"The market was changing," he observed. "The market had been made on making it smaller, because you could replace people with all that this thing does. Then our marketing department told us the things we knew—people wanted a machine with more power, that goes faster, with less cost, same weight, and same length or shorter. But they also told us the product had become not one of necessity—for use instead of hiring a bunch of guys with shovels—but a product of choice."

There were serious competitors cropping up in the 1980s, Lynnes found. "We didn't pay enough attention to the competition. All the things that started the market—turkey barns, hog barns—didn't exist anymore. They were automated in other ways."

While Bobcat Company continued on its path, its new competitors were adapting their own designs for new uses. One of these competitors introduced a skid-steer loader in the early 1970s that had a longer wheelbase. "We spent ten years criticizing them for making a long machine," Lynnes said.

MISSION TO JAPAN

While Melroe's team studied the Toyota threat and considered its options, leadership at Clark pressed it to find some means of preventing another Waterloo in the industrial market. Clark installed a new president, Jim Rinehardt, who had been president of General Motors of Canada. Rinehardt, CEO Bob Spolum recalled, was aware of what had happened in the fork-lift market with Toyota, and then Komatsu, grabbing market share from Clark. When Rinehardt became aware that Toyota was planning an assault on the skid-steer market, he summoned Spolum to Clark's headquarters in Buchanan, Michigan.

Rinehardt asked Spolum if the company was aware of the potential Toyota problem. Spolum told him the company had picked up a Toyota loader and had run it through teardown, and

127

BOBCAT REPORTS:
THE MELROE MISSION TO JAPAN

>> *After hearing that Toyota planned an assault on the skid-steer loader market, Melroe Company assembled a team of 33 people to go on a mission to Japan. Above is the team members' report chronicling the trip and their activities. "The Melroe Mission to Japan" helped usher in new concepts in both manufacturing and engineering.*

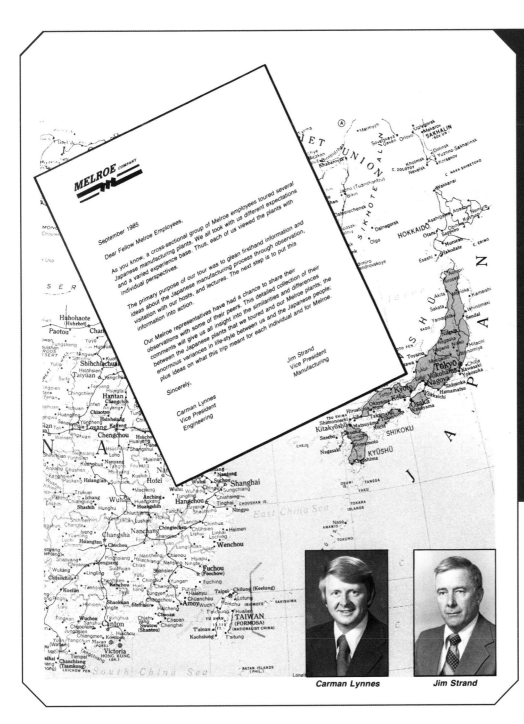

Melroe Groups Visit the Land of the Rising Sun

It was the first airplane ride for some, the first overseas flight for most, and a mission of learning for all. It was the "Melroe Mission to Japan" on which thirty-three Melroe employees joined together in mid-May to explore ideas, techniques, and a vastly different culture. This cross section of people toured Japanese manufacturing plants, talked with Japanese citizens, ate a variety of Japanese food, and got to know each other and their competition better.

As Charles Orn, Bobcat General Assembly in Gwinner, says, "For us to compete with the Japanese, we will have to adopt some of their techniques. Their system is A #1." The groups spent many hours touring a variety of manufacturing plants, including Kubota, TCM, Mitsubishi, and Mazak.

"I feel that the trip provided us with the understanding of the Japanese system — their competitive threat to us. Seeing them in their workplace hopefully will result in certain approaches here at Melroe," comments Orlan Loraas, Manager of Product Engineering at Gwinner. As every American company is faced with competition, so is Melroe and the Melroe Bobcat. This group met face to face with the country that has so fiercely competed with many U.S. products.

LaVerne Colby, Purchasing Manager in Gwinner, adds, "I think that after this trip, some of our people now realize the reality of the competition. We are having to get smarter. We realize that the world is getting smaller. Whoever does the best job is the most successful." Small groups in which the Melroe travelers have shared their observations and ideas have gotten together in both Bismarck and Gwinner. For those seeing firsthand the Japanese factory system, the message is clear. Leo Bosch, Area Manager in Bismarck sums it up this way, "I hope that I can put together my information to help Melroe be a better company in which to work."

For ten days, these Melroe emissaries observed a lifestyle far removed, yet in some ways similar, to our own. "It's imperative that everyone live and cooperate on the same train of thought over there," says George Jury, Senior Manufacturing Engineer in Bismarck. "They are brought up to be conformists." Continues Arlin Meier, Bismarck welder, "We can't expect to compare with the Japanese philosophy because the two cultures are so vastly different."

This second issue of the "Mission to Japan," offers observations made by our travelers on a variety of subjects. Although the group members each offer their individual thoughts, collectively the group is in agreement on key issues. According to Larry Albright, Development Engineer in Gwinner, "If you weren't a believer (in the Japanese threat to our economy) before you went, you were when you returned."

And Alvin Brandt, welder in Gwinner, summarizes, "The competition is so fierce. The Japanese are seeking market share at any expense . . . even if it is not profitable."

This second issue is filled with photos and comments from Melroe's 33 employees who toured Japanese manufacturing plants.

>> *At left, a memo explains the group's reason for traveling to Japan and the importance of their findings. Above, the company publishes a special newsletter section on the group's trip to Japan to distribute internally.*

September 1985

Dear Fellow Melroe Employees,

As you know, a cross-sectional group of Melroe employees toured several Japanese manufacturing plants. We all took with us different expectations and a varied experience base. Thus, each of us viewed the plants with individual perspectives.

The primary purpose of our tour was to glean firsthand information and ideas about the Japanese manufacturing process through observation, visitation with our hosts, and lectures. The next step is to put this information into action.

Our Melroe representatives have had a chance to share their observations with some of their peers. This detailed collection of their comments will give us all insight into the similarities and differences between the Japanese plants that we toured and our Melroe plants: the enormous variances in life-style between us and the Japanese people; plus ideas on what this trip meant for each individual and for Melroe.

Sincerely,

Carman Lynnes
Vice President
Engineering

Jim Strand
Vice President
Manufacturing

Carman Lynnes   *Jim Strand*

was "pretty damn concerned about it." What would they do about it? "We're going to fight them and take them head on," Spolum recalled of his response to Rinehardt.

Rinehardt told Spolum he was worried.

"Well, can you give me any advice?" Spolum asked.

"All I can do is pay your salary. If you can't get it done, I won't pay your salary," was Rinehardt's response to Spolum.

Spolum got the message and gathered Bobcat's team together. Their task was to come up with a plan to handle the Toyota threat. They agreed their company didn't know the Japanese culture or manufacturing process. They also agreed the company had to learn those things, partly because of what had happened in the automotive business, but mainly because of what they'd seen firsthand in the lift truck businesses. The first step, they decided, would be a mission to Japan.

As the idea began to gain steam, executives realized that it couldn't be a single employee, or even a few from the company's top executive levels. It would have to be a multidisciplinary group, drawing from every part of the organization, that could learn about the Japanese production process and find out what, if anything, was missing in North Dakota.

Choosing the employees that would go to Japan, however, would take a bit of finesse. Spolum realized that choosing 33 people, some from off the factory floor, would lead to jealousy and charges of favoritism, even though employees would come from all across the company—Gwinner and Bismarck, machinists, engineers and salespeople alike.

An equally thorny problem was the union leadership of the Gwinner plant. Spolum realized that regardless of whether he or the union representative chose the mission members, it might preclude a productive team experience. "So we decided we won't pick them—we'll let them pick themselves, we'll let the departments decide who's going to go." Spolum also invited the union leader to go along on the trip, to send the right message.

By putting the selection of mission members to a vote, Melroe's leadership learned an important lesson about their

>> *Bobcat at home: the skid-steer loader helps the city of New Orleans prepare for the 1984 World's Fair.*

>> *Melroe employees belonging to "The Melroe Mission to Japan" team arrive at the Tokyo airport and stand in line for the currency exchange counters. For some, it was their first time ever flying.*

employees: the people the individual departments chose as international representatives were the very ones management would have picked. "They took the cream of the crop," Spolum said. "They selected the same people we would have."

The company prepared their missionaries for the trip in big ways and in small ones. Half of them had never been on an airplane, and "probably 90 percent had never been outside the country." Their 10-day itineraries were booked for 12 to 14 hours each day, filled with plant tours and visits to Japanese families. They would be charged with paying attention, taking notes, and coming back home to spread the word on how the company could take on its biggest challenge yet.

WHEN IN TOKYO...

From North Dakota, the flight to Tokyo seemed to take forever, and on arrival the time-zone change made midday the perfect time to fall asleep for eight hours. But employees were on the move from the time they landed—and their eyes were opened wide by the differences in Japanese culture and in the way they built industrial products.

Those 33 employees detected myriad differences in the way everyday Japanese life differed from their own in Gwinner.

John Henline, an engineer from the Gwinner plant, reported, "Japan has very strict vehicle inspection laws, so mostly new vehicles were on the road. They must keep their cars new and nice looking to pass inspection." The group found out that to own a car in Japan, you must first prove that you have a place to park it. Taxes increase on cars the older they are to encourage consumers to purchase new ones. And Paul Brinkmeyer from the Bismarck operation discovered that "owning a car in Tokyo is a pain, because everything costs so much for parking, maintenance, etc."

As for the food in Japan, many workers were unimpressed. Upon returning to North Dakota, Richard McIntyre, a brake operator in Bismarck, said, "They can have their food. I tried the sushi, but didn't care for it. We did have a couple of good steaks, though."

It was inside the factories, however, where the team from North Dakota saw how their own operations could be improved—or at least, reorganized—to better compete with the up-and-coming Japanese model of just-in-time manufacturing.

"The biggest difference was in the assembly line and the flow of materials from station to station. Where we use forklifts they use hoists and conveyors," observed Wally Vollmers, an area manager in Bismarck.

"The plants were clean and well painted. Layout of the machinery was easier for the worker — in lines rather than groups," added Darrel Salberg, from the tape-lathe-machine shop in Gwinner.

"Their plants were more automated than ours. Their housekeeping is 100 percent better than ours. They had better storage areas. Material on the lines is a lot handier . . . everything is right there," recalled Charles Orn, Bobcat general assembly.

The very physical design of the factories played a role in the Japanese companies' assembly techniques, and nearly every visitor reported back on the cleanliness in and around the Japanese plants.

"Even though the land is valuable, the plants had ample property," said Wally Vollmers, Bismarck.

"The cleanliness just about knocked you over," added Alvin Brandt, from Gwinner.

"Their housekeeping is the biggest, [most] striking thing. It was evident in all of the plants. They are proud of their cleanliness; it has to do with the way that they live," concluded Jim Messmer from Gwinner. "They even have carp living in their waste water ponds to test for cleanliness."

Managers who went on the trip made their own observations—and gradually, the Japanese advantage became discernible. "All of a sudden we started to see how they did this," Riebe said. "It wasn't the design of the part, it was the design of the cell that manufactured it. Where we had one person working on one machine they had one person working on six machine tools. Where we transferred a basket of parts from machine to machine, they took one part and took it from machine one to two to three, then put it in the basket instead of moving the parts around the plant," he says. "They had made great strides in efficiency, great strides in how they used their people."

The factory also didn't store a lot of spare parts. Instead, it depended on a network of smaller—even micro—suppliers who regularly dropped off parts at the factory as needed. "We saw parts that we thought might be very expensive, that were produced by very small companies—mom and pop companies," Riebe said. "These companies would have small half-ton pickups, would drive right into the plant, unload their parts, and drive right away."

"Our common knowledge went right out the window," Riebe continued. "We had to be just-in-time, not just-in-case."

What the team had observed would forever change how the Melroe division did business. The entire just-in-time philosophy was adopted and adapted by the North Dakota company from the Japanese model. Machine shops were converted so a single employee was responsible for several stages of production, taking a part through processes to better ensure a rejection rate of zero, which meant all the proper steps had been completed and the part was dimensionally and qualitatively perfect.

"We brought that philosophy back home. And our factories responded. And our manufacturing engineers did a hell of a job on bringing in the proper equipment to do so. We even went to a paint system that cost $3 million, but we finally got an automotive finish on our loaders."

"We drove the competition nuts," Riebe smiled.

"It was tremendously effective," Bob Spolum agreed. It was, in all likelihood, "the most effective thing we've ever done."

COURTING DIPLOMACY

While the mission to Japan would give Melroe's employees a unique insight into a new way of building machines, no amount of manufacturing change alone could overcome the threat of Toyota and other Japanese products. So while workers from Gwinner and Bismarck and Fargo flew to Tokyo for a 'round-the-world education, CEO Bob Spolum took another tack—a diplomatic one—to help ensure Melroe's progress would be put to the test on a level playing field.

"I went the other direction," he recalled. "I said, 'We've got to go to Washington and bend the ear of someone down there.' So, we got an audience with our two senators and one representative, Byron Dorgan. I flew down to Washington to talk to our three congressmen and the Department of Commerce. They were very much aware of the problem we had early on, and they were aware of exactly where we were coming from," Spolum explained.

While he visited with Rep. Dorgan—now one of North Dakota's two U.S. Senators—Dorgan let it slip that he was to have an audience with the trade minister of Japan in the next week. While Dorgan promised to raise the Toyota issue, another representative waved them off, saying the problem was with the Japanese currency, the yen, and nothing could be done.

Spolum's final visit in Washington was with Senator Quentin Burdick—whom Spolum recalled fondly. "What a gentleman. We sat and talked with him and described our problem."

Burdick's advice was for Spolum to fly to Tokyo, where a colleague from Montana would arrange a meeting with the U.S. ambassador to Japan, Mike Mansfield. And when Spolum arrived, he was greeted with open arms. "We walk into a huge room, and here's an old guy in his 80s, but sharp as a tack. 'Damn it's nice to see people from the Midwest over here!' he said. 'How would you guys like a good cup of American coffee?'"

Spolum couldn't have been prepared for the good news he was about to hear. After describing the situation in the lift-truck industry, he implored Mansfield for help. "All we want is a level playing field," he recalled telling Mansfield. "We don't want them to come in and undercut price and buy business from us. We can't fight them fairly on those kind of grounds."

"Well, a very good friend of mine is Mr. Toyoda, the chairman of Toyota," Mansfield answered. "I will contact him and explain this situation to him."

The message Spolum took home to Fargo was clear: the Japanese "would not pull any funnies, and would come into the market on a so-called level playing field."

>> *Da zvidanye! Bobcat arrives in Moscow and helps clean up Red Square, five years before the fall of communism.*

>> *In the era before Germany reunited, Bobcat loaders help repair and reconstruct the country's former (and now current) Reichstag parliament house.*

LET THE GAMES BEGIN

In a letter to the Melroe team written on his return, Spolum conveyed the importance of the mission to the rest of the company. "To remain in first place over our competition, it will take a team effort. It will take you, and me, and our sales network joining in solid force to thwart the imminent Japanese invasion into our market. Those 33 who saw firsthand what our competition can do have given us information with which to meet this challenge," he wrote.

"People came back full of enthusiasm on what we need to do equipment-wise," Spolum recalled. "And I came back with the message that at least we were protected in a sense."

The sense of gravity had spread far and deep within the company. Keeping their company competitive took on an urgency—and became a matter of pride. LaVerne Colby, a purchasing manager in Gwinner, wrote in an employee newsletter, "I think that after this trip, some of our people now realize the reality of the competition. We are having to get smarter. We realize that the world is getting smaller. Whoever does the best job is the most successful."

By 1986, the way forward for the company was clear. And it responded.

"Bobcat did a complete turnaround in how we did business," Grover Riebe observed. "We became sophisticated in equipping our plants, machining centers, robotics, training programs. We got very involved in quality, took a hell of a lot of cost out of the unit, and froze prices for 10 years. That drove the industry nuts because we didn't have price increases. During this period of freezing our prices, we came out with better quality and made more money.

"We brought this Japanese concept to Gwinner and made it work," he concluded.

>> *Marketing to the European customer meant meeting them where they worked—and played. Bobcat Europe even sponsored a continental basketball team at one point.*

But the most interesting part of the mission to Japan story would take place six years later, in August, 1992. Clark had sold its lift truck business in the interim, because it hadn't made money for 8 or 10 years, Spolum recalled. And in that late summer of 1992, the team learned it had won a battle many American companies had lost: Toyota announced it would be leaving the North American skid-steer market.

"Because we were cost competitive, we drove them out of the market," Riebe said. "And they haven't been back."

BOBCAT IS A WORK SAVER

An essential part of today's skid-steer loader market is the owner-operator. Whether in landscaping, contracting, or demolition, a whole new customer base has developed in the past two decades as the original uses for skid-steer loaders—cleaning barns and the like—disappeared.

Jim Kertz said the transition from agricultural to industrial company was essentially completed in the late 1980s and early 1990s. Kertz, who had returned to the company's headquarters in 1982 after a stint in European operations, recalled the company had started to recognize that the brand was in transition, and that owner/operators were becoming an ever-larger piece of their business.

"That almost coincided with the huge growth in the skid-steer market," Kertz recalled. "And the development of additional models that went from one to—God, I don't know how many there are now."

"I think the last thing in our mind was to do anything to alienate the dealer organization."

It was Bobcat dealers who tied the growing cadre of owner/operators to the Bobcat Company. Larger rental companies like Hertz would often rent for longer periods, but it was the local dealers and short-term rentals that proved to be the best advantage for the Bobcat brand. "These people would come in and rent a machine, then the dealer had a prospect built right in," Kertz explained.

The wave of new customers and users eventually earned its own moniker—BYOB, for "Be Your Own Boss" or, from the dealers' perspective, "Buy Your Own Bobcat." Often, Kertz said, they would start out as subcontractors. "Suddenly there were two machines, they'd hire somebody, buy a truck, and

Bobcat Team of Worksavers

>> *Bobcat issued its first* **WorkSaver BobCatalog** *edition in 1992, covering the breadth of its lineup, from skid-steer loaders to compact excavators to articulated loaders.*

135

get rid of the trailer. Some of these folks became very well-to-do business people," he recalls.

Bobcat also started a publication for customers and prospects called *WorkSaver*—an apt description for what the Bobcat loader did for these customers. For over thirty years, *WorkSaver* has brought owner/operators the latest information on Bobcat's innovations and business models—and users like themselves who have built their own business foundations one skid-steer loader at a time.

THREE GENERATIONS OF BOBCAT

Louis and Steve Klumker were two *WorkSaver* stars. The Klumker family bought a new Bobcat loader nearly every year for 33 years. The loaders were a part of the family business, which provided services to contractors, farmers and homeowners.

Louis, 79 years old at the time of the *WorkSaver* article, had started his business in 1967 with the purchase of an M600 loader. His son grew up and progressed from operating loaders on weekends with his father to helping run the business.

The Klumkers' business evolved, and they landed large contracts like assisting in the construction of a $300 million desert resort with lagoons, swimming pools, and golf-cart paths. Klumker's business also took him to neighboring states including New Mexico, Utah, and California to do mine-shaft cleanup, timber removal, and concrete-slab construction for microwave towers.

>> *Louis Klumker was featured on the cover of WorkSaver magazine with his fleet of Bobcat 743 skid-steer loaders. The Klumker family bought a new Bobcat loader nearly every year for 33 years.*

MODELS

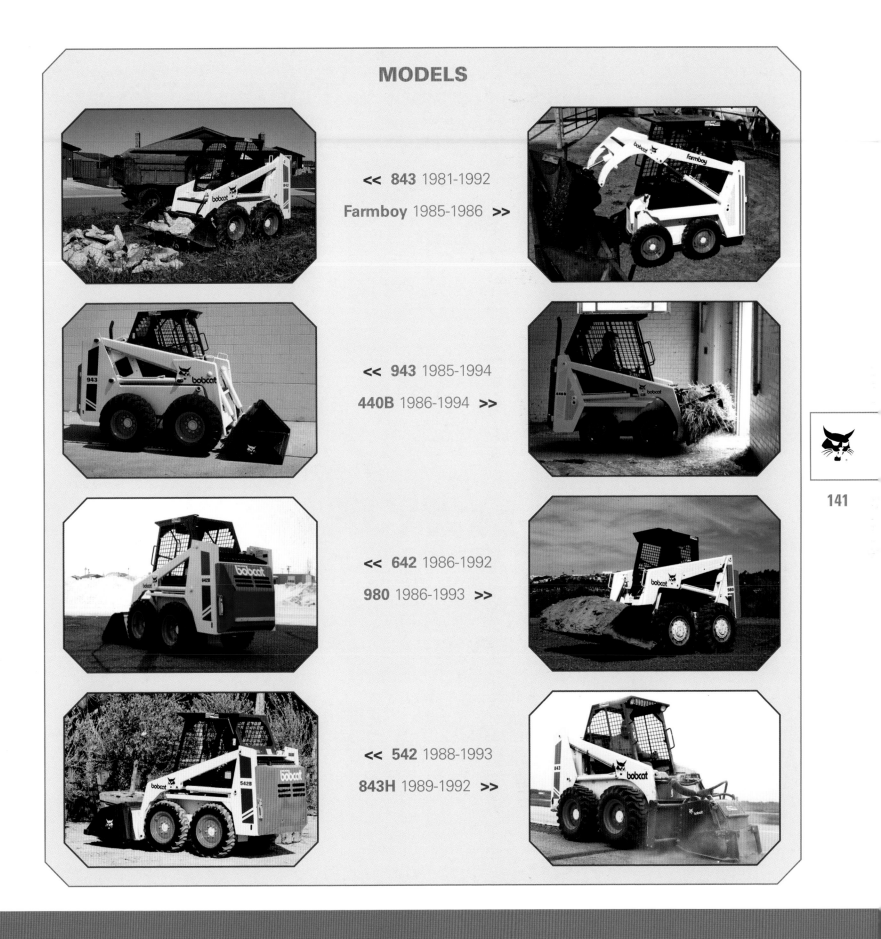

<< **843** 1981-1992

Farmboy 1985-1986 >>

<< **943** 1985-1994

440B 1986-1994 >>

<< **642** 1986-1992

980 1986-1993 >>

<< **542** 1988-1993

843H 1989-1992 >>

141

>> The range of Bobcat machines covered a broad spectrum of uses, from construction to demolition to landscaping and excavation. Here, Bobcat machines lay in wait at a St. Louis dealership.

>> A range of Bobcat trenchers—models T114, T108, and T136—was added to the company's lineup in 1986. The trencher line, however, was divested by 1991.

had acquired in 1986, were divested in 1991; the Kirschmann Spra-Coupe, purchased in 1973, was sold in 1998.

Entering the modern era, the Bobcat loader reigned as king of the skid-steer market. As a Clark division, the Melroe Company and its Bobcat brand was the biggest company in North Dakota, and the state's largest manufacturer, employing nearly 2,220 North Dakotans in Gwinner and Bismarck, as well as Fargo—site of the company's headquarters since 1976. Along the way, the Bobcat loader had bred a multitude of enthusiasts—major industrial companies and owner/operators alike—who built allegiance to their skid-steer loaders as they built their businesses.

The Bobcat loader had won them all over—just as it had won over the Clark Equipment Company in 1969. By 1995, it had essentially taken over Clark's profit statements. The Bobcat brand was a winning business, and in an age of ever-larger conglomerates—some of which dwarfed Clark in size—it was only a matter of time before the company became the target of another takeover.

TIMELINE

1983
Bobcat introduces a beefed-up 1080 Feller Buncher with planetary drives for better performance and durability.

1984
Melroe's new "Flying M" logo signifies its change from a division of Clark Equipment Company to a business unit of the company and the return of the Melroe Company.

1985
Bobcat's sales rose to $195 million; new axle-cell robots enter the Bobcat production system.

1986
Bobcat sources a compact excavator from European and Japanese companies and realizes an important new product has joined the lineup. Eventually the company will produce its own units in Bismarck, North Dakota, U.S.A.
Bobcat acquires the Midmark Trencher Company of Dayton, Ohio, and enters the trencher business.

1987
Bobcat Europe hosts the "winning combination" dealer and press event in Brussels to introduce the expanded Bobcat line.

1988
Fortune magazine names the Bobcat skid-steer loader to its "America's Best" list—100 American-made products that represent the best of their kind, anywhere in the world.

1989
Bobcat's transportation fleet numbers 38 tractor-trailers as it drives growth across the country.

1990
Bobcat launches the 50 Series skid-steer loaders. In addition to durability and performance improvements, a new diagnostic and monitoring system, known as the Bobcat Operation Sensing System, or BOSS, is introduced.

1991
Fortune magazine names the Bobcat skid-steer loader to the "America's Best" list for the second time.

1992
Bobcat launches the 7753 "lift and carry" loader, which uses a multiple linkage lift arm to create a vertical lift path, greater capacity, and longer wheelbase.

1993
Bobcat's third generation of compact excavators enters production, while the 1600 and 2410 articulated loaders and the 980 skid-steer loader are dropped from the lineup.
Bobcat introduces the first comprehensive operator training course for skid-steer loader.

1994
Bobcat sales soar to $604 million.

>> Hydraulic breakers, like that found on this 442 excavator, are big business in the construction field.

Leader
of the Pack

Bobcat was a brand on the move. By the early 1990s, sales had climbed to over half a billion dollars a year, and new variants on the traditional skid-steer loaders were finding strong acceptance in construction, landscaping, and all kinds of other industrial situations. Dealer rental programs were generating not only profit, but new owner sales, too. The little white machine had become an American icon, and seemingly, no construction site was complete without one.

The growth that the Bobcat loader had fueled at Clark Equipment Company had saved that company from years of losses. Through many fiscal periods, it had kept Clark in the black, according to former Melroe executives. The downside to this success? Clark's multiple businesses were now ripe for acquisition, with the Bobcat model line the crown jewel in the assortment of industrial equipment makes.

It didn't take long. In 1995, Clark Equipment Company, and its Melroe division, were acquired by Ingersoll-Rand Company of Woodcliff Lake, New Jersey. Ingersoll Rand, or IR, was at the time a leading maker of construction equipment and industrial machinery, and counted more than 40,000 employees.

The acquisition came as Ingersoll Rand executed a philosophy not unlike Clark's in the late 1960s—acquire

>> In 1995, Ingersoll-Rand Company purchased Clark Equipment Company and its Melroe business unit. The tailgate on this Bobcat 773 skid-steer loader dumping a load of snow illustrates the Ingersoll Rand influence on Bobcat after the acquisition.

brands with strong resonance and top market share in their niches. Today, Bobcat loaders are part of an empire that includes the Club Car golf cart, Hussman, Thermo King

<< *The turn of the millennium shows the Bobcat line's rapid growth, which reflects Ingersoll Rand's influence on the company.*

refrigeration products, Schlage locks, and a wide variety of Ingersoll Rand-branded lines of compressors, generators, air tools, and other construction equipment.

Right away, Bobcat began to contribute to the Ingersoll Rand bottom line. In its first full year as an IR subsidiary, Bobcat had a record performance, helping to boost the parent company's sales to more than $7 billion.

In turn, Ingersoll-Rand Company provided additional research and development resources, allowing a greater focus on product innovation. The company encouraged global manufacturing development, including the acquisition of several products and manufacturing plants in France and the Czech Republic. The result was a series of new product lines added under the Bobcat brand over the following decade.

The Bobcat lineup had narrowed its focus over the course of the most recent decade. Even back in 1980—indeed, back to the very start of the Melroe Company—engineers and marketers realized that no product had an eternal shelf life.

>> *The versatile Toolcat™ 5600 utility work machine is especially popular for clearing snow from parking lots, walkways, and bike paths.*

"Some markets have disappeared on us, or at least started toward disappearing," Orval O'Neil said at the time. "One is unloading boxcars. I think there is a good reason for that. I heard on the radio the other day that one of the Minneapolis grain terminals no longer takes boxcars. It will only take grain in hopper cars. They won't unload boxcars.

"Are there any other markets like that that have disappeared simply because of technological changes? I know that some are heading that way to a minor degree. Dairy barns with slatted floors, hog barns with slatted floors, there are other markets of that nature that are going to have to be replaced with something else or the market is eventually just going to get more away from it. Where we're going to be superseded is by something more sophisticated."

As the Melroe era dissolved into the Clark era, then Clark into Ingersoll Rand, the list of machines carrying the Bobcat logo was winnowed. In 1993, management had culled the articulated loaders from the line. These loaders offered slim profits and the Bismarck plant that built them faced difficulties doing so efficiently. The large 980 skid-steer loader met the same fate, at the same time. In their places, the company expanded compact excavator production in Bismarck, where it remains today.

Melroe's windrow pickup and agricultural businesses had been sold off in the 1980s. And when the Spra-Coupe crop sprayer was sold to AGCO Corporation in July of 1998, it marked a fundamental shift in the Bobcat brand's marketing strategy. From its roots as a farm hand, essentially cleaning barns, it had become a multi-purpose machine, still capable of cleaning barns but also of grading earth, laying sidewalks, digging pools, and doing any number of tasks to meet the contemporary owner-operator's needs.

BUILDING THE BRAND

As Bobcat Company sales exploded in the 1990s, brand awareness was on the rise. And as the image of the Bobcat brand spread around the world, marketers and dealers alike recognized how other companies were getting more customers—by moving peripheral merchandise along with the product itself.

Roger Fischer, parts merchandising manager for Bobcat at the time, witnessed the explosive growth in this other side of

>> *The Bobcat Company added articulated loaders to its product line in 1981 with the Bobcat 2000 and this 2000 rough terrain forklift (RTF). Just a little more than a decade later, management pulled the machines from the Bobcat line.*

the Bobcat business. In showrooms today, Bobcat machines are proudly on display, as they have been for 50 years. But a marked change in the past decade has put Bobcat merchandise to the fore, for customers who already own a machine as well as those who aren't quite ready to put themselves at the controls.

Fischer's career started in the newsroom of the West Fargo *Pioneer*, and nearly took him from that newspaper to Cleveland. But "I was tired of chasing fire engines and ambulances," Fischer recalls, and when advertising manager

Ferd Froeschle called him in 1974 and offered him a job, Fischer couldn't turn it down. Working with Froeschle, Fischer joined the Bobcat team as a writer, editing the company newsletter *Bobcat's Pajamas*, and helping to plan most of the company's meetings.

Fischer's focus turned to branding the tires, oils, and other ancillary products that joined Bobcat machines on the dealership lot and in the showroom—everything from scale models to rakes and shovels to clothing.

"About 1998 things really broke loose with the brand strategy," Fischer said. "Merchandising was identified as a major player in the company in terms of growing the dealers' profit. As we tell everybody, sales will sell the first one, service and parts sell the rest of them."

Scale models became a large component of Bobcat's brand identity. Dealers also increased their success by improving the layout of their stores. "We showed them a vision of what a store should look like," Fischer said. "Gloves, hydraulic oil—it's an impulse buy. If you get it out from behind the counter, people will buy it," he said. Clothing is a big business too, Fischer added. And a big increase in Bobcat-themed merchandise sales in the Internet era came through www.BobcatStore.com, where people can shop for Bobcat gear without leaving home.

BUILDING A GLOBAL PLATFORM

The growing number of dealers around the world brought dramatic changes to the Bobcat production system. Machines are designed for easy service and reliable operation. And the very way Bobcat machines are built has been transformed over the past decade, allowing technology to be transported around the world to new factories.

When Grover Riebe entered the company's manufacturing ranks in June, 1966, the Melroe Manufacturing Company was making its first inroads into European and Australian sales. Forty years later, Riebe, the director of manufacturing technology, works with operations in Gwinner and Bismarck—and in France and the Czech Republic, as well.

Transporting technology is no easy task. By benchmarking the best ideas and building around them, however, changes to the Bobcat manufacturing process became easier to move from factory to factory, Riebe said. From the old-fashioned

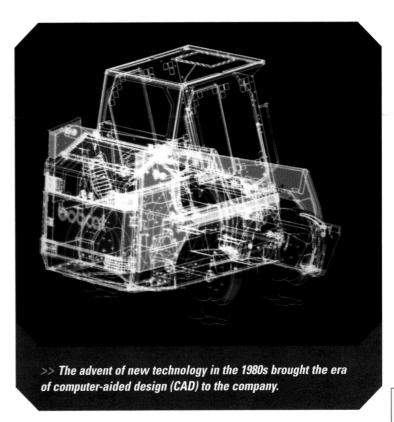

>> *The advent of new technology in the 1980s brought the era of computer-aided design (CAD) to the company.*

method in which individual workers installed a single piece on a machine, or performed a single task, Bobcat moved to cellular manufacturing, meaning that a single employee supervises several steps in a process, ensuring high quality. Robotic assistance is often involved, and the manufacturing cells themselves are designed to a specified size so ideas can be transferred to production facilities in Europe—or back home to North Dakota.

In much of the Bobcat production system, parts and structures pass from one cell to the next with no direct intervention unless it's needed, Riebe explained. "The operator becomes a manager, and there are time frames where they have to go in and make changes," he says. "They're managing a cell. Now we have areas where one operator is managing three or four cells."

As methods of manufacturing move from one continent to another, they might require modification. Bobcat engineers learned that differences in rules and regulations might dictate slight changes to process, but they did not have to affect the overriding principles of production. The French and Czech factories, for example, have different designs for

>> *Robotics have been integrated into the Bobcat production process since the early 1980s. The machine's frame is welded almost entirely by robots.*

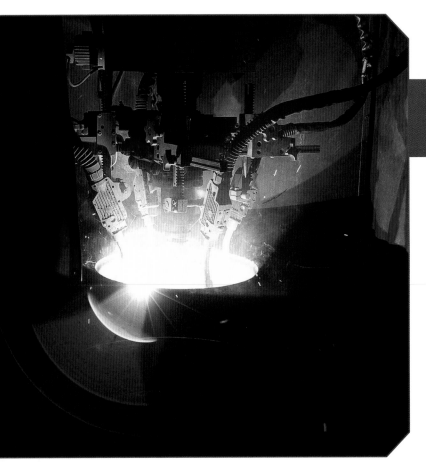

>> *A skid-steer loader's wheel rims are welded at the company's Gwinner plant.*

manufacturing cells that are close, but not exactly identical, to those installed in Gwinner or Bismarck, because of European Union approval of certain robots and electronics. European work rules also dictate various procedures, and the size of some manufacturing cells. To overcome the differences, Bobcat brings its European engineers to Gwinner and Bismarck to show the intent of the manufacturing process, Riebe said, so that "engineers in both Czech and France understand what we're trying to do."

Especially in the Czech Republic, there have been big challenges in teaching the new methods to a workforce trained outside North Dakota. "The big challenge is to get them to see the possibilities," Riebe said, "how to take them to the next level without having to make all the same mistakes we did."

BOBCAT AT HOME—AND AT WAR

Part of Bobcat's appeal, even in the Czech Republic and in France, or anywhere else it is sold, is that it is a uniquely American success. For the past generation, news headlines have warned about the departure of manufacturing from the United States to countries with less costly labor pools, such as China or India. But Bobcat's work force has adapted to the globalization of industry and responded with high-quality products built at a profit—something that hasn't escaped the most influential business newspaper in the world.

The *Wall Street Journal* recently identified a handful of companies that have succeeded not only in keeping their production base in America, but in building almost cult-like reputations among their owners. Among the companies cited was Viking, which builds high-end stoves and ranges in a factory deep in the heart of the Mississippi Delta, an area

>> *Bobcat accepted its mission in the war on terror when machines were dropped into Afghanistan for reconstruction work.*

HONORED BY AG ENGINEERS

Bobcat's impact on the industrial world has been huge, but even in the days of the original three-wheel loader, the machine that would become the skid-steer loader had the power to change the way farming was done. Because of that impact, the American Society of Agricultural Engineers, in 2004, awarded the skid-steer loader status as a historic landmark of agricultural engineering with the following dedication:

"Brothers Cyril and Louis Keller designed and built the first small, lightweight, three-wheel, front-end loader in their machinist-blacksmith shop in Rothsay, Minnesota. A local farmer wanted to mechanize cleaning manure from his obstacle-filled, two-story turkey barn. The machine, first used in 1957, was able to turn completely around within its own length.

"Melroe Manufacturing Company, Gwinner, ND, purchased the rights to the Keller loader and hired the Kellers to continue development of the loader in 1958. The first four-wheel, true skid-steer loader was the M400 manufactured in 1960. The "Bobcat" name was first used in 1962 on the M440.

"The skid-steer loader's utility comes from its turning ability and its many versatile attachments. Bobcat pioneered

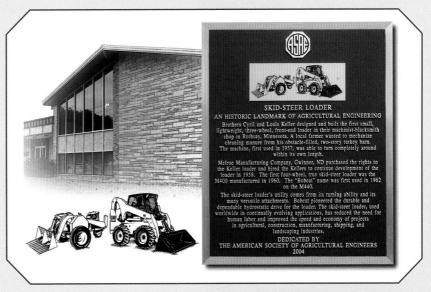

the durable and dependable hydrostatic drive for the loader. The skid-steer loader, used worldwide in continually evolving applications, has reduced the need for human labor and improved the speed and economy of projects in agricultural, construction, manufacturing, shipping, and landscaping industries."

traditionally known more for its poverty and turbulent race relations than its manufacturing expertise.

Bobcat is another home-grown success story, according to the *Journal*. In an article entitled "Still Built on the Homefront," *Journal* reporter Timothy Aeppel identified the qualities that have made Bobcat a success at home and around the world:

The Bobcat factory dominates Gwinner. In its two cavernous assembly halls—ancient machine presses alongside the latest robot welders—three shifts working 24 hours a day, five days a week, churn out more than 40,000 machines a year.

Bobcat has exploited its location to keep a finger on the pulse of its core market of small landscaping and construction contractors, helping it quickly develop and ship products. Also, the company's rural setting, executives say, has bred the kind of culture where problems are solved with the can-do, make-do ethos of the farm.

Bobcat, which operates another large factory in Bismarck, is North Dakota's largest exporter, shipping $550 million in machines to all corners of the globe annually. Meanwhile, the

>> **Bobcat loaders are working at the Crazy Horse Memorial to help sculpt the mountainside statue of the Indian leader.**
Pictured above: **Dennis Jenner, Doug Jenner, and Daryl Hanson.**

company's steady growth—11% a year for the last decade—helps explain why North Dakota is one of only three states that consistently added manufacturing jobs over the last three years. The other two aren't classic industrial regions either: Nevada and Alaska.

"A friend of mine calls it the Swiss army knife of the construction equipment world," says Charles Yengst, president of Yengst Associates, a market-research firm in Wilton, Conn.

Mr. Yengst notes that other much bigger equipment manufacturers make similar products, including Caterpillar and Dutch-based CNH Global. But the undisputed leader in the niche for compact loaders remains Bobcat."

While the business world admires Bobcat's record for growth, its neighbors applaud its corporate citizenship. Whether it's in the state of North Dakota—where Bobcat donated a machine to the Bismarck zoo for cleanup use—or

pitching in at national parks from shore to shore, Bobcat has given back to the state, to the Midwest, and to the country.

In neighboring South Dakota, for example, Bobcat's donation of a machine to the Crazy Horse Memorial helped speed up construction on the monumental sculpture being carved into the Black Hills. The project had been using an M610 loader for more than 25 years when the company and local dealer Jenner Equipment approached it with an offer of a new 873 loader. The hydrostatic loader has a 2,400-pound capacity, thanks to its 73-horsepower diesel engine, and is now at work on the site, helping with on- and off-the-mountain carving as the project enters a new phase. Though still in progress the monument receives more than one million visitors each year.

Across the country, Bobcat recently participated in the annual "Renewal and Remembrance" day at the Arlington

>> Snowblowing is a snap with the all-wheel-steer Bobcat A300, a recent addition to the company's portfolio.

>> In military service, this 763 Bobcat skid-steer soldiers on as it augers a hole in the ground.

>> Bobcat loaders in the Army: here, a machine reports for duty at Fort Campbell, Kentucky.

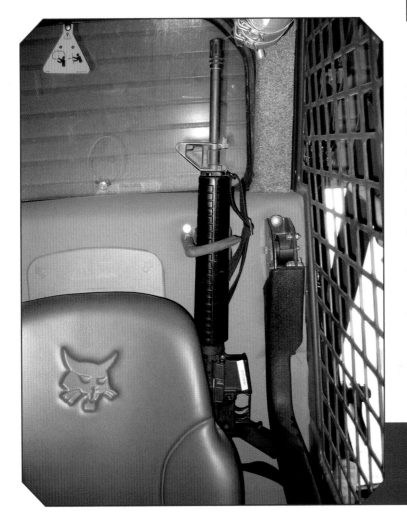

>> This enlisted Bobcat enthusiast brings the Bobcat message to the rebuilding of Iraq.

National Cemetery, across the Potomac River from the nation's capital. As an associate sponsor of the Professional Landcare Network (PLANET) event, Bobcat donated the use of an A300 all-wheel-steer loader, an S250 skid-steer loader, and two Toolcat 5600 Utility Work Machines. Bobcat machines were put to work spreading lime over the cemetery's nearly 250 acres, and renovating the landscape around the visitors' center.

And as the war on terror continues, Bobcat's military presence in Iraq and Afghanistan continues as well. Bobcat machines have been used in military applications for decades, and these are the few machines not to wear Bobcat's traditional white paint. From digging trenches to moving pallets of military gear, the Bobcat lineup works alongside our soldiers, helping them complete their missions safely.

>> Attachments and accessories come often from ideas that Bobcat owners share with the company. This home-made gunrack on a military loader might not make it into production, though.

>> Bobcat utility vehicles are favored by groundskeepers for their cargo-carrying capability.

>> Bobcat utility vehicles are also used by hunters. This 2100 utility vehicle wears camouflage paint.

BOBCAT OF TOMORROW

While the Bobcat Company plans and markets—and dealers sell—the skid-steer loaders of today, the company is already preparing the next generation of machines.

The development team considers all aspects of the Bobcat experience—ease of use, cost of manufacturing, safety—as it works toward the launch of the next skid-steer loaders. "Customers can tell you what they want, but they won't tell you what the next leap in technology will be or should be," said global product manager Paul Anderson.

Cross-functional teams are created to get the inside information on what operators of all types of Bobcat machines want by asking and observing them. "What are you doing, and what can we do to make your job easier?" Anderson asked. "We ask them and watch them. We go out on job sites, and watch what they're

>> Bobcat loaders help the world go green—the machines are often found at recycling centers, where they move material being processed for reuse, like these aluminum cans.

TRADE SHOWS

BAUMA 2007

>> Bobcat has a significantly higher profile at international trade shows like Bauma, demonstrating the scale of Bobcat's presence worldwide. Held every three years at the Munich Trade Fair Center in Germany, Bauma attracts more than 500,000 visitors from about 190 countries.

CONEXPO-CON/AGG 2005

>> Here, Bobcat exhibits at CONEXPO-CON/AGG, which attracts more than 125,000 visitors from the construction industry every three years in Las Vegas. With 2,000 exhibitors spread across 2.1 million net square feet of indoor and outdoor space, CONEXPO-CON/AGG is the largest trade show in the United States.

GREEN INDUSTRY EXPO 2004

>> Pictured is the Bobcat booth at Green Industry Expo, the premier landscaping trade show that brings together professionals from the landscaping and grounds maintenance markets. Held annually, visitors can view equipment in the exhibit hall, as well as test drive machines during outdoor demonstrations.

![A giant 4000-ton press in a factory building]

>> *This giant 4000-ton press in Gwinner is used to form 1/4-inch tailgates (seen in the foreground) as well as other large stampings, such as overhead guards for loaders. The machine has footings 30 feet deep and stands 30 feet tall, and the building that houses it needed to be constructed around the press after it was installed.*

>> *The assembly line at Bobcat's Gwinner, North Dakota, factory has seen dramatic changes since the modern era of robotics and just-in-time production began.*

doing. If the machine is sitting and they're doing something else," that's the first indication of a potential direction for development, he added.

One major area that will be addressed in the new machines is operator comfort, Anderson indicated. "Drivers always like to be clean and comfortable. Many of today's operators who have experience with the older models prefer the traditional hand levers and foot pedals we've used since day one. But new operators grew up using computer-game joysticks, and we need to satisfy their needs and wants, too. So, we offer both now. Some folks run foot pedals part of the day, then switch to the hand controls."

Work has begun on expanding military applications of the company's lineup, with innovations like easy-change electronic controls that make unmanned operation simpler and less costly. In the past the military spent up to $100,000 to convert Bobcat loaders to unmanned remote-control operation. In 2007, Bobcat's engineers will reduce that cost by about 90%. The plug-in radio remote control electronics will help the company meet a military plan to switch most machines and vehicles to unmanned operation.

Product testing continues year-around in Arizona at the company's proving grounds—a location that has become a real plus as a complement to North Dakota's tough winters. The Tucson test track has accelerated product development, and speeded up durability testing. "Bobcat will continue for the next 50 years doing what the company did for the last 50 years, it will continue to listen to the customers and build what they want and need," said Anderson."

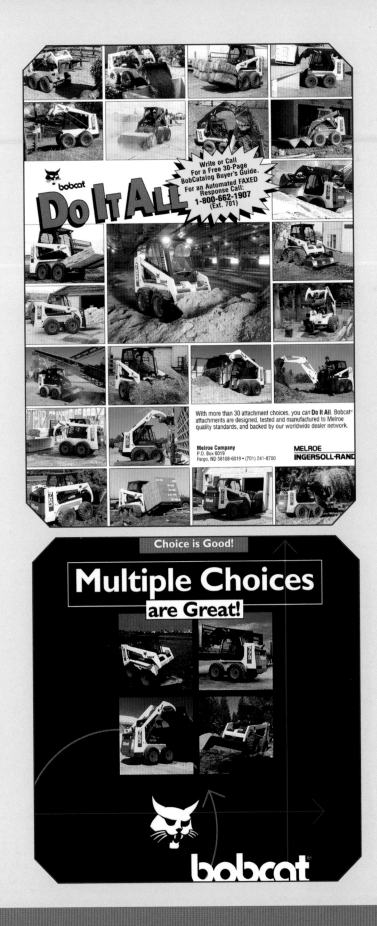

Do It All

With more than 30 attachment choices, you *can* **Do It All**. Bobcat® attachments are designed, tested and manufactured to Melroe quality standards, and backed by our worldwide dealer network.

Melroe Company
P.O. Box 6019
Fargo, ND 58108-6019 • (701) 241-8700

MELROE
INGERSOLL-RAND

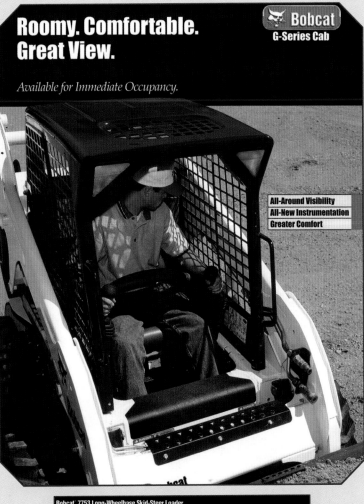

Roomy. Comfortable. Great View.

🐱 **Bobcat**
G-Series Cab

Available for Immediate Occupancy.

All-Around Visibility
All-New Instrumentation
Greater Comfort

175

Choice is Good!

Multiple Choices are Great!

bobcat®

Bobcat® 7753 Long-Wheelbase Skid-Steer Loader

🐱 **bobcat**

7753
Long Wheelbase SSL

The Ideal Lift And Carry Machine.

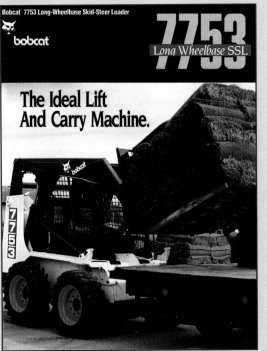

BOBCAT'S EXTREME HOME MAKEOVER

No, it's nothing as radical as a nose job or a facelift for the world's most popular skid-steer loader. The Bobcat extreme makeover took place in the summer of 2006, as the machine and the company were called upon to help out a Minot, North Dakota, family in an episode of the hit ABC television series, *Extreme Makeover: Home Edition.*

In the summer of that year, producers of the show, which stars loud-spoken home-improvement celebrity Ty Pennington, had settled on the Bliven family of Minot, North Dakota, as the recipients of a complete renovation to their home. The family's second son Aaron had been born with cerebral palsy, and the family had started a special-needs Little League baseball team for Aaron and other disabled children. As Aaron grew, his wheelchairs outgrew the family home—just as father Bill suffered two heart attacks and could no longer lift his son.

Kellers' exhibit at the Sargent County Museum in Forman, North Dakota.

BOBCAT "FIRSTS"

1958: Louis and Cyril Keller team up with Melroe brothers to develop first production three-wheeled loader, forerunner to the skid-steer loader.

1960: Melroe Manufacturing Company creates world's first skid-steer loader—the M-400.

1962: First use of "Bobcat" trademark.

1970: Bob-Tach™ quick-change attachment system first used on the M970 and M600.

1970: M970 "Big Bob" is first hydrostatic skid-steer loader.

1971: M371 "Mini Bob" is world's smallest skid-steer loader.

1973: "Bobcat Kid" is first skid-steer loader safety video.

1981: Bobcat seat bar secondary restraint system.

1987: Bobcat 980 is world's largest skid-steer loader with 4,000-lb. rated operating capacity.

1989: Bobcat manufactures first compact excavator in United States.

1990: Bobcat Operation Sensing System (BOSS®), state-of-the-art diagnostic and monitoring system.

1993: First Bobcat operator training course introduced.

1994: Bobcat Interlock Control System (BICS™).

1999: Deluxe instrumentation panel displays seven different languages with keyless start and vital loader operating information.

2001: Bobcat A220, world's first loader to combine all-wheel steer and skid-steer operation.

2003: Toolcat™ 5600 utility work machine is first vehicle of its kind.

2003: Bobcat 430 and 435 zero house swing (ZHS) excavators.

>> *Bobcat loader cabs offer a selectable joystick controls (SJC) option and deluxe instrumentation panel. In 2003, Bobcat introduced the SJC option for skid-steer and compact track loaders, enabling operators to choose preferred joystick control pattern for loader steering and hydraulic functions. A deluxe instrumentation panel, which was introduced in 1999, displays seven different languages with keyless start and vital loader operating information.*

2003: Selectable joystick controls (SJC) option for skid-steer and compact track loaders enables operator to choose preferred joystick control pattern for loader steering and hydraulic functions.

2004: The MT52 mini track loader is introduced with first ride-on platform that may be easily detached for walk-behind operation.

>> In 1994, Bobcat introduces the Bobcat Interlock Control System (BICS™), which prevents operation of the lift, tilt, and traction drive functions unless the operator is seated with the seat bar lowered.

2004: Bobcat 2200 is first utility vehicle with IntelliTrak® drive system, equipped with automatic locking differentials that engage immediately when a wheel loses traction.

2005: Speed management feature enables operators to match loader travel speed to operation requirements.

2006: Bobcat 2300 utility vehicle with RapidLink™ attachment system.

>> In 2003, the Toolcat™ 5600 utility work machine is introduced and is the first vehicle of its kind. It incorporates all the best features of a utility loader, pickup truck and attachment

183

MARKETING HISTORY

Perspective of Donovan Kolness, Flint Communications

Bobcat Company and its products have grown and evolved over the decades, but one thing has remained constant — its marketing message.

"Actually, that's one of the secrets to their success — it's still the same philosophy," says Donovan Kolness, executive vice president of Flint Communications. "We push the toughness, versatility, and agility of the equipment, so that message has stayed consistent all the way through."

As the company added compact track and mini track loaders, compact excavators, telescopic tool carriers, utility vehicles and utility work machines to its product line, Flint Communications had to get the Bobcat message out to a growing number of markets. Kolness, who has worked on the account since 1972, has witnessed firsthand the company's growth. For example, when he first started on the account there were fewer than a half-dozen equipment models to promote. Since then, he has been involved in creating advertisements for more than 200 new Bobcat models.

In the early years, Kolness says internal sales promotions were instrumental to catapulting Bobcat into the compact equipment leader it is today. "Keeping dealer salesmen pumped up and excited, that's what I think was a major part of their success," he says. "The ads were delivering a message, but the internal sales promotions really vaulted Bobcat beyond its competitors."

Because many of the equipment innovations Bobcat incorporated were the result of customer recommendations, it wasn't hard for Flint Communications to sell the message that Bobcat was a company that listened to its customers. We're

Donovan Kolness

consistently leading the industry," Kolness says. "Bobcat never stood still. They have constantly strived to improve the product."

What also has helped the company's marketing efforts is that signature styling features have survived the many different models that have come off the manufacturing line. For example, Kolness says the basic white frame, charcoal cab, and orange tailgate and rims remain easily distinguishable trademarks of Bobcat loaders. "They were able to pull those styling features through all of the new product lines, which has really kind of held that branding together," he says.

>> Melroe self-propelled loader advertisement, 1959.

>> This mid-1960s Melroe ad articulated the Bobcat machine selling advantage word-for-word.

>> Ads like this 1970 one touted the man-replacement element of the Bobcat loader.

>> Melroe Bobcat compact loader advertisement, 1969.

>> This ad was part of "Bobcat Manpower" campaign during the 1970s.

>> This 1992 campaign promoted the "Bobcat System."

>> A new 751 F-Series Bobcat skid-steer loader ad promotes 1983 pricing in 1992.

>> This 1998 ad campaign continued to promote the versatility of Bobcat machines and attachments.

>> This 2004 advertisement went back to the basics of promoting the versatility of Bobcat machines.

>> Bobcat attachments advertisement, 2002.

SPECIFICATIONS M-371 LOADER

SPECIFICATIONS

THE MELROE **M-371** BOBCAT®

SMALLEST LOADER ON THE MARKET!

MELROE DIVISION · CLARK EQUIPMENT COMPANY · GWINNER, NORTH DAKOTA

>> *This 1971 promotional piece played up the compact size of the M371 loader.*

LOADER
The Melroe BOBCAT—a four-wheel drive self-propelled loader — expanded Melroe sales into national and international markets. Because it is compact, maneuverable and highly versatile, it is used in a wide range of industries . . . construction, fertilizer, mining, foundry, forestry and agriculture. A variety of attachments increases its versatility.

HYDRAULIC HARROWEEDER
Although not the first MELROE product to be marketed, the Harroweeder has been responsible for much of the growth of the Company. A unique tillage tool, the Melroe Hydraulic Harroweeder does double duty: Preparing seed beds and weeding row-crops.

WINDROW PICKUP
The Melroe windrow pickup for combines was originally developed before World War II by E. G. Melroe, founder of the company. It is still a major farm equipment item, marketed in North and South Dakota, Minnesota, Montana and Canada.

AUTOMATIC RESET PLOW
This is a recent Melroe acquisition, obtained through purchase of Reiten Manufacturing Company, Cooperstown, North Dakota. In rough, rocky ground each bottom on the Melroe Reset Plow yields automatically . . . to speed plowing, eliminate share breakage.

CHISEL PLOW
The Melroe Chisel Plow has five exclusive features, including four-bar spacing for better trash clearance and a balance-bar system which maintains positive control of tillage depth.

>> *This 1969 company literature piece pointed out Melroe's versatile agricultural product lines.*

189

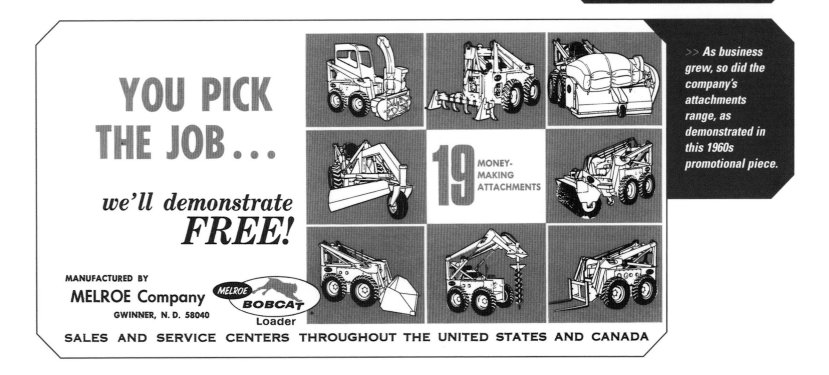

YOU PICK THE JOB . . .

we'll demonstrate FREE!

19 MONEY-MAKING ATTACHMENTS

MANUFACTURED BY
MELROE Company
GWINNER, N. D. 58040

MELROE **BOBCAT** Loader

SALES AND SERVICE CENTERS THROUGHOUT THE UNITED STATES AND CANADA

>> *As business grew, so did the company's attachments range, as demonstrated in this 1960s promotional piece.*

BOBCAT PROMOTIONAL MARKETING TO DEALERS

Not only did Melroe Company market to customers, but it also marketed to its dealers—getting them excited about sales promotions such as the Melroe Bobcat key tags. This was just one of many dealer promotions that Melroe Company launched during the 1960s and early 1970s to help build the Bobcat name and brand. Other promotions included the "Live Action Advertising" wearables program and the "Something for the Girls" Bobcat pin promotion following the Chandler, Arizona, sales meeting.

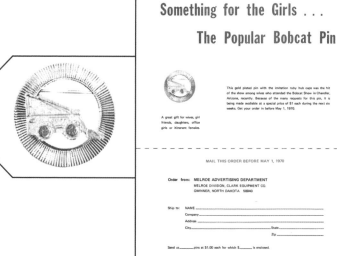

190

Ferd Froeschle
Bobcat Advertising Guru
As told by Jim Kertz, former Bobcat Company president and CEO

Ferd Froeschle

t'd be hard to find a person at Bobcat Company who hasn't heard of the legendary Ferd Froeschle, the company's advertising manager from 1965 to 1981. The late Froeschle (pronounced "freshly") continues to be admired by many in his profession — not only for the marketing skills he possessed, but also for his natural ability to bring creativity, passion, and enthusiasm into everything he did.

"He was the kind of guy who lived his work and loved his job, and he had great loyalty to his company and co-workers," says Jim Kertz, former Bobcat Company president and CEO who was first hired by Froeschle. "He had the unique ability to take his work seriously, but he was able to inject it with humor and infectious enthusiasm."

What also made Froeschle so successful and well respected was his ability to change with the times. "He knew things were changing and needed to be adapted to, and many times, he was able to anticipate the changes," Kertz says. "His creative juices were always flowing. Everything inspired an idea or project and he was able to pass along that enthusiasm to his staff."

The Melroe BOBCAT . . . Lovely little homewrecker

The Melroe BOBCAT Loader is a lot of fun to play with . . . but really serious about her work. Demolition contractors can hardly keep their hands off her. She can make a shambles out of a ground floor kitchen in seconds or go up 20 stories to wreck an entire bachelor pad in minutes. Barely 5 feet high and 54 inches across the hips, the M-600 can really maneuver in those hard-to-get-at places.

You wouldn't carry her across the threshold but the M-600 weighs a mere 3,269 lbs. . . . so hoist her to the roof or sneak her up on the elevator. Give her a big bucket or Ho-Ram attachment and the Melroe BOBCAT will take down walls and dump debris over the side in a hurry. And you could get attached to 19 other easy-on at-

tachments. She's no pushover either . . . positive four-wheel drive gives sure traction on any surface.

Cut your hand labor costs in half — finish every demolition job ahead of schedule . . . and below your bid projections. Just for fun, call your local Melroe BOBCAT dealer for a FREE on-the-job demonstration. Or send us a love-letter direct.

MELROE COMPANY
GWINNER, NORTH DAKOTA 58040
Please send me free illustrated literature and price list on the Melroe BOBCAT Loader . . . and details on Free demonstration.

Firm Name _____
Address _____
City _____
State _____ Zip _____
Sales and Service Centers throughout the United States and Canada

---

CLARK EQUIPMENT

CLARK EQUIPMENT COMPANY

Melroe Division

Gwinner, North Dakota 58040
Telephone: 701/678-6363
Telex: 29-229

Dear Bobcat fans:

Here it is - the "Bobcat Sex Machine"! Almost since the first day the Bobcat loader rolled off the assembly line, people have been asking for a scale model. We now have a limited supply of these 700 Bobcat models and we're prepared to give them to our dealers at a special introductory price. Just $120 for a carton of 20 units. As the literature sheet in this month's Kit explains, there are almost as many uses for these models as the real Bobcat loader!

The "It Works" story this month is on nurseries; one of those great Bobcat applications. Some of our dealers in Florida are burning up the road delivering machines into this market. They tell us that the nursery owners are just waiting for a machine to replace their wheelbarrow and shovel. If you haven't looked at this market, now's the time!

We're sending you some more of those catchy little Bobcat Classifieds. Feel free to rewrite them to fit your own sales areas. Classifieds are a great way to keep your dealership name out in front of the public - at little cost. If you're already using some of the classifieds we've sent you in the past, we'd like to know if you're getting results. Drop us a card.

Tom Stuart's people have included a Service Training schedule in this month's Ad Kit. If you have men that need training, sign them up today.

Sincerely,

Ferd Froeschle

Ferd Froeschle
Advertising Manager

FF:kh

You've Been Clamoring For "IT" For Years.

THE BOBCAT SEX MACHINE

Here "IT" Is . . . At Last!

TAKE OUR LITTLE MODELS, PLEASE!

ORDERS MUST BE IN BY JUNE 15, 1975 FOR SPECIAL INTRODUCTORY PRICE ONLY.
SEX MACHINE SUPPLY IS LIMITED. (NO FOOLING!)

Melroe Advertising Department
Melroe Division
Clark Equipment Company
Gwinner, North Dakota 58040

Thank you. We've waited long enough. Send us _____ carton(s) of the 700 Sex Machines. $120 per carton of 20 units. Forget the certificates, we'll do our own.

Dealership _____
Address _____
City _____ State _____ Zip _____
Signature _____ Date _____

Only one of these Melroe Bobcat Models is yours . . .
The BOBCAT 700 Hydrostatic Loader

Sold in 20 unit cartons
Only $120 per carton . . .
LIMITED SUPPLY. Honestly!

THE FAMOUS MELROE MOVIES

Dating back to as early as the 1950's, Melroe Company began using film to promote the harroweeder and to later convey the Bobcat Story to customers. The company produced several movies and television advertisements, including "Bobcat Square Dance," "Bobcat A-Go-Go," and educational videos about the equipment manufacturing process, operator safety tips, and the different markets and applications. The movies just weren't for Melroe employees' eyes. For years, the company shared the films with dealers, customers, schools and others in the public through a free lending library.

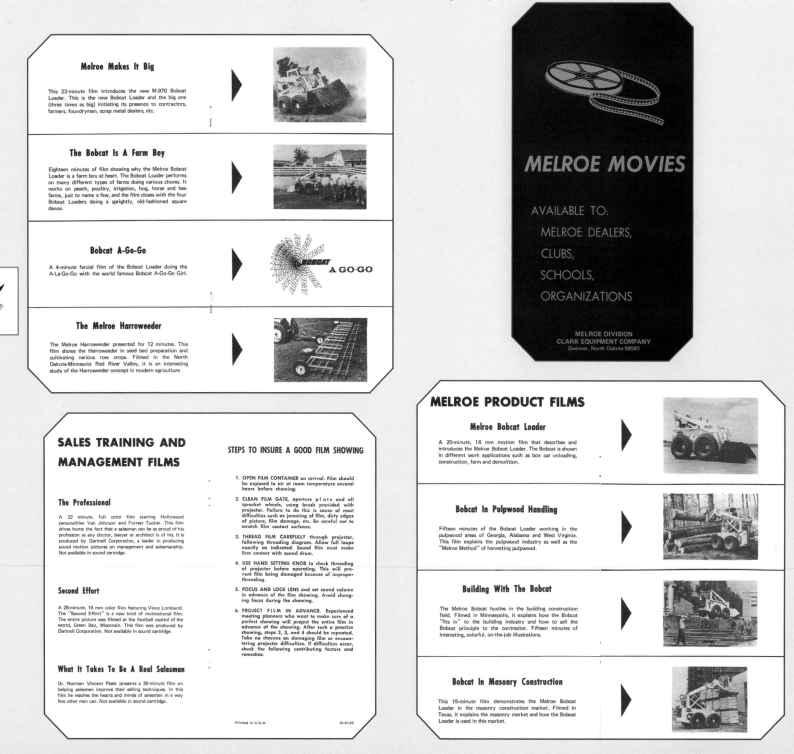

Melroe Makes It Big

This 22-minute film introduces the new M-970 Bobcat Loader. This is the new Bobcat Loader and the big one (three times as big) initiating its presence to contractors, farmers, foundrymen, scrap metal dealers, etc.

The Bobcat Is A Farm Boy

Eighteen minutes of film showing why the Melroe Bobcat Loader is a farm boy at heart. The Bobcat Loader performs on many different types of farms doing various chores. It works on peach, poultry, irrigation, hog, horse and bee farms, just to name a few, and the film closes with the four Bobcat Loaders doing a sprightly, old-fashioned square dance.

Bobcat A-Go-Go

A 4-minute farcial film of the Bobcat Loader doing the A-La-Go-Go with the world famous Bobcat A-Go-Go Girl.

The Melroe Harroweeder

The Melroe Harroweeder presented for 12 minutes. This film shows the Harroweeder in seed bed preparation and cultivating various row crops. Filmed in the North Dakota-Minnesota Red River Valley, it is an interesting study of the Harroweeder concept in modern agriculture.

MELROE MOVIES

AVAILABLE TO:

MELROE DEALERS,

CLUBS,

SCHOOLS,

ORGANIZATIONS

MELROE DIVISION
CLARK EQUIPMENT COMPANY
Gwinner, North Dakota 58040

SALES TRAINING AND MANAGEMENT FILMS

The Professional

A 32 minute, full color film starring Hollywood personalities Van Johnson and Forrest Tucker. This film drives home the fact that a salesman can be as proud of his profession as any doctor, lawyer or architect is of his. It is produced by Dartnell Corporation, a leader in producing sound motion pictures on management and salesmanship. Not available in sound cartridge.

Second Effort

A 28-minute, 16 mm color film featuring Vince Lombardi. The "Second Effort" is a new kind of motivational film. The entire picture was filmed at the football capitol of the world, Green Bay, Wisconsin. This film was produced by Dartnell Corporation. Not available in sound cartridge.

What It Takes To Be A Real Salesman

Dr. Normen Vincent Peale presents a 30-minute film on helping salesmen improve their selling techniques. In this film he reaches the hearts and minds of salesmen in a way few other men can. Not available in sound cartridge.

STEPS TO INSURE A GOOD FILM SHOWING

1. OPEN FILM CONTAINER on arrival. Film should be exposed to air at room temperature several hours before showing.

2. CLEAN FILM GATE, aperture plate and all sprocket wheels, using brush provided with projector. Failure to do this is cause of most difficulties such as jamming of film, dirty edges of picture, film damage, etc. Be careful not to scratch film contact surfaces.

3. THREAD FILM CAREFULLY through projector, following threading diagram. Allow full loops exactly as indicated. Sound film must make firm contact with sound drum.

4. USE HAND SETTING KNOB to check threading of projector before operating. This will prevent film being damaged because of improper threading.

5. FOCUS AND LOCK LENS and set sound volume in advance of the film showing. Avoid changing focus during the showing.

6. PROJECT FILM IN ADVANCE. Experienced meeting planners who want to make sure of a perfect showing will project the entire film in advance of the showing. After such a practice showing, steps 2, 3, and 4 should be repeated. Take no chances on damaging film or encountering projector difficulties. If difficulties occur, check the following contributing factors and remedies:

Printed in U.S.A.   M-4125

MELROE PRODUCT FILMS

Melroe Bobcat Loader

A 20-minute, 16 mm motion film that describes and introduces the Melroe Bobcat Loader. The Bobcat is shown in different work applications such as box car unloading, construction, farm and demolition.

Bobcat In Pulpwood Handling

Fifteen minutes of the Bobcat Loader working in the pulpwood areas of Georgia, Alabama and West Virginia. This film explains the pulpwood industry as well as the "Melroe Method" of harvesting pulpwood.

Building With The Bobcat

The Melroe Bobcat hustles in the building construction field. Filmed in Minneapolis, it explains how the Bobcat "fits in" to the building industry and how to sell the Bobcat principle to the contractor. Fifteen minutes of interesting, colorful, on-the-job illustrations.

Bobcat In Masonry Construction

This 15-minute film demonstrates the Melroe Bobcat Loader in the masonry construction market. Filmed in Texas, it explains the masonry market and how the Bobcat Loader is used in this market.

The *WorkSaver Story*

As told by Leroy Anderson, marketing communication manager

If there's one magazine that embodies the toughness of Bobcat compact equipment, it's *WorkSaver*, which has grown to become the voice of Bobcat customers.

WorkSaver magazine has been a part of the Bobcat Company marketing program since late 1976, when it was conceived as an alternative for reaching the large and prosperous farm market. Dealer demand quickly resulted in an "industrial" edition of WorkSaver, which alternated with the "farm" edition for a monthly mailing schedule by 1978.

After several years, the farm and industrial editions merged and the mailing schedule was reduced to six times a year. With the rapid decline of the agricultural market—and the strengthening of the construction/industrial/rental markets in the early 1980s—*WorkSaver* was restructured and the editorial mix refocused into its current format of four larger issues a year.

Today, *WorkSaver* magazine provides more than just product information. The magazine features customer profiles, job stories, and tips articles to help Bobcat customers excel in any market, whether it be construction, landscaping, rental, grounds maintenance, agricultural, industrial, or personal use. Today *WorkSaver* is printed in English and Spanish, and reaches both current and prospective customers in the United States, Canada, Australia, New Zealand, New Guinea, and the Pacific Islands.

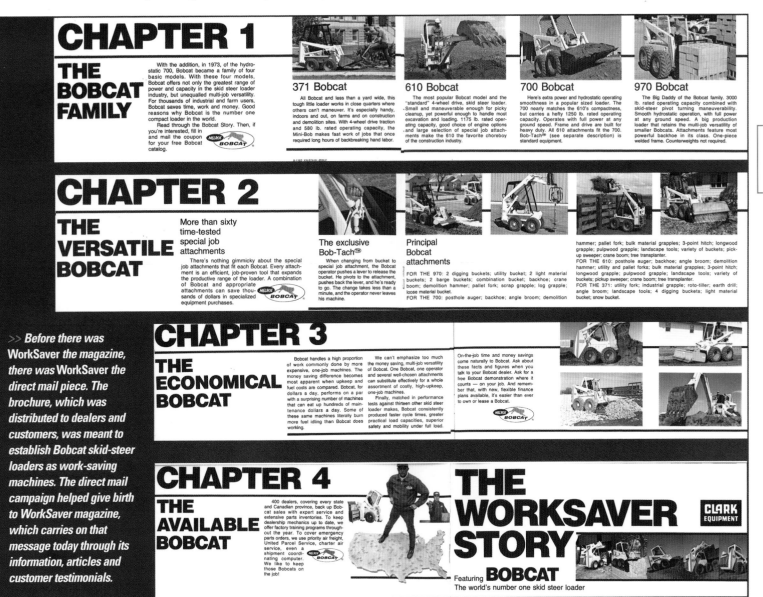

>> *Before there was* WorkSaver *the magazine, there was* WorkSaver *the direct mail piece. The brochure, which was distributed to dealers and customers, was meant to establish Bobcat skid-steer loaders as work-saving machines. The direct mail campaign helped give birth to* WorkSaver *magazine, which carries on that message today through its information, articles and customer testimonials.*

193

Volume 1, Number 1

work**saver**

Great Farm Dogs... Page 4

>> *Volume 1, Number 1, 1977 — Inaugural issue of WorkSaver magazine with a focus on "Great Farm Dogs"*

bobcat

work**saver**

Fall 1984

Melroe: A Proud Name Returns
Solar's Future Uncertain: Clouded By Controversy
There's More Than One Way To Finance A Bobcat

>> *Fall 1984 — The Melroe name returns (legendary Mount Rushmore parody cover)*

bobcat

work**saver**

Spring 1987

Landscaping Adds Value To Sites

Duluth Is Rebuilding

Winter In A Rocky Mountain Resort

>> *Spring 1987 — Showcasing the ever-growing Bobcat family, including new trenchers and excavators*

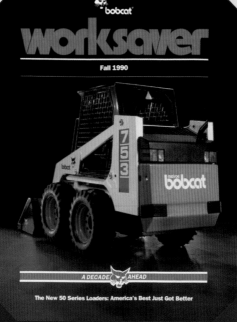

bobcat

work**saver**

Fall 1990

A DECADE AHEAD

The New 50 Series Loaders: America's Best Just Got Better

>> *Fall 1990 — Unforgettable 50-Series introduction ("America's Best Just Got Better")*

bobcat

work**saver**

Special Section: The Bobcat System

>> *This Summer 1992 cover wrap introduces the "Bobcat System" (loader/excavator team) to the world.*

WORKSAVER

195

1977-1986

WorkSaver editor Paul Posel has overseen the magazine since 1990. He retired his full-time position in July 2007.

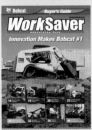

WORKSAVER

1997-2007

197

Reflections

What has Bobcat meant to you?

We asked dealers, retirees, and long-time Bobcat employees what the organization, products, and people involved meant to them. The specific answers varied, but the theme was the same: opportunity. Whether an individual was in production, traffic, sales, or part of the management team, the reflections pointed to self-betterment, an improved lifestyle, and a chance to raise a family close to home—all with a great sense of pride in what they helped the Bobcat brand to become.

The variety of design challenges presented by a machine as compact as a Bobcat loader, and the opportunity to successfully engineer solutions and see them develop from concept to prototype to production is most rewarding. I am very fortunate to have had a career at Bobcat.

Larry Albright
Product design engineer, 1972–2006

Service and reliability: It's the world's best compact loader! Financial security: Many friends and neighbors here and in towns for many miles around work at the plant. Many workers at the factory are second generation.
Economy: Bobcat is a major customer for many vendors who supply engines, belts and hoses, computers, wiring harnesses, glass, seats, welding supplies, steel—the list is endless. There are many more support industries such as transportation and utilities. Bobcat workers support churches. Area schools depend on student enrollment and

taxes generated by Bobcat. Workers also buy products and services from local businesses.

Norman Alme,
Dealer, 1959–1996;
plant worker, 1996–2002

It's been my whole life. I came out of college and went to work for the company, and they've been really good to me . . . To this day, my kids still yell "Bobcat Alert" if we're driving down the road and spot a machine.

Paul Anderson
Product development and sales, 1972–Present

It gave me an opportunity to contribute my knowledge and my efforts to building a great product, which gave me a chance to grow professionally. It provided a workplace in rural North Dakota, which is a great place to live, enjoy the outdoors, and raise a family.

Harold Beckstrom
Product Engineering, 1972–2006

Next to God and family, Melroe was Earle's life. The shows (dealer meetings) were hard work, but fun, and he was working with a great bunch of men and women. Melroe meant everything to him. I still have the machine that he bought me!

Ruby Benson
Wife of Earle Benson, Truck driver, 1968–1994

It was the best job I ever had. Every morning was different . . . Every morning I was glad to get up and go to work.

Bud Borke
Field sales, 1957–1989

Bobcat has given my family and my extended families an opportunity to contribute and recognize all our differing jobs as a series of challenges and growth that we're all very proud to be a part of.

Dorene Brown
Assembly, 1979–2004

I've just got to say it was just a heck of a lot of fun. I wish everyone who works could have as much fun as I did in those last 20 years, because it would sure make companies a lot better.

Jim Brust
Sales, 1968–1989

Entering the Bobcat Company was like entering a great worldwide family with roots in North Dakota. Marketing the Bobcat machines was more than selling a product—it was selling an entirely new working concept, which is now recognized and implemented worldwide. I'm very proud to be part of the early pioneering team.

Paul Cuypers
International sales and marketing, 1968–1998

Opportunity . . . I kind of wanted to be a lawyer. Thank God I didn't get to be one.

Eugene Dahl
Company management, 1950–1970

Working at Melroe was a true blessing for farmers. We will be forever grateful for the opportunity to have a better living, and for our means to educate our five children.

Enne Enervold
On behalf of Bert Enervold, machinist, 1965–1980

It wasn't just my career, it was my family . . . . We (at Bobcat) were a family.

Roger Fischer
Marketing, merchandising, and after-market parts, 1974–2006

I remember the people. I think I was blessed with the opportunity to work with some of the best talent and most highly motivated people anyone could ask for.

Jack Fowler
Manufacturing, 1973–2004

We had the privilege of living a dream.

Doug Freitag
Sales, 1972–2004

Bobcat (Melroe) provided my family and me with a comfortable living. It was a business family that cared about us.

Earle Gackle
Ag division, 1965–1998

Opportunity to meet good people, work with good people, and laugh with good people . . . . People are intensely proud of what they've done here.

Dick Gerriets
Service, 1972–Present

Bobcat enabled my family and me to have a great life. It allowed me to become a man. Coming from a poor farm family, Bobcat helped me become much more than I ever dreamed I could. Thank God for Bobcat, the Melroe brothers, and the Kellers.

John Griggs
Assistant service manager, 1967–1991

The product he sold was true and good.

Bernice Grosz
Writing about Ed Grosz, Sales, 1965–1982

199

I enjoyed my job very much. Working on the assembly line building Bobcat machines was a great part of my life even though I was blind. Those years were the best of my life, and it was the best job I ever had. I was treated like a king.

Emil Gunsch
Assembly, 1972–1989

There isn't a year that goes by that I'm not grateful for the years I spent at the Bobcat factory. The friends that I learned to respect and hold dear will always be part of my life.

Eugene Halvorson
Assembly, 1967–1988

Over the years, we were rewarded with excellent benefits . . . not just monetary . . . friendships, a sense of accomplishment, respect, and pride. But mostly it was an opportunity for Ardell to put his heart and soul into a company he believed in.

Doreen Hansen
Writing about Ardell Hansen, traffic manager, 1957–1982

Bobcat and the people were my life, I guess, for about 36 years, along with my personal family. It was a great occupation.

Galen Hanson
Sales, 1964–2000

I not only delivered Bobcat machines around the country and Canada; I also had the privilege of working the sales meetings for the company, so I got to work with and know the sales and office people. They taught me how to work with different people with different training, and I learned a lot. Bobcat was the best thing that could have happened to me.

Richard Hanson
Truck driver, 1971–1997

I worked for Melroe Company for just over 20 years, and my years there were very good years. I learned a great deal about the business world. During those years, I also saw the ups and downs of the company—more ups than downs. Most importantly, I made so many good and lifelong friends. We were truly like a close-knit family, and I feel fortunate to have worked there during that time.

Becky (Paczkowski) (Nayes) Hebert
Executive secretary, sales and marketing, 1979–1999

200

Bobcat has meant a great deal to me and my family. I was the last man hired by E. G. Melroe before his death, and in 1958, I machined parts for the first self-propelled loader to be made at the Melroe Manufacturing factory.

Gerald Hegle
Machinist and Quality Control department, 1955–1987

Security . . . We were one big happy family, and Bobcat was very good to their people.

Fred Hein
International Marketing, 1968–1989

As time went along, and we got to be more famous in the world, it was very gratifying to see that we were satisfying customers out there. And wherever you would go, people would know the name Bobcat; if you had the Bobcat name on your jacket or shirt, they would identify with it, no matter where you were in the world, be it Europe or Asia.

John Henline
Product Engineering, 1970–2002

When I think back to the great people that made up the Bobcat organization, they were almost always very humble, passionate people that were most interested in the company being successful. If the company was successful, they knew that they would have many career opportunities. In today's world, it seems that there are far more people that are mainly interested in their own career success, and the company success is secondary. The Bobcat order of priority was to, first, do what is right for the customer, second, do what is right for the company and, third, do what is right for the individual employee. Bobcat people who "bleed white" maintained this order of priority and values. They also created a culture of innovation and fun.

Chuck Hoge,
Controller, 1989–1996, *Company president, 1996–2002*

I grew up with the Melroe family. Irving Melroe and I were the same age and we went to school together. I worked on their farm and started with the factory as a part-time welder—the only welder. Then in 1950, I started full-time, and later as the company grew, I was plant superintendent. It was great to be associated with Bobcat from the start and see it grow with the many good people we hired and the good product we built.

Allen Holmstrom
Manufacturing, 1950–1982

We were just like one big happy family . . . It was a very friendly company, with good bosses, and there was never a day that I disliked my job.

Carolyn Hopewell
Executive administrative assistant, 1963–1994

It was my first job out of college . . . For me, it was my start. It helped me reach my goal of owning my own farming operation.

Gordon Irwin
Product Engineering, 1959–1968

The company was growing continually, and we just grew along with it . . . We didn't even realize we were growing.

Carolyn Jacobson
Traffic, 1965–2006

Great times. Great places. Great people.

Robert Janssen
Engineering and Service, 1972–1991

Bobcat meant a steady income with raises that put food on the table and bought the other things a family with six children needs.

Max Jensen
Assembly and Welding, 1966–1995

We were "scraping the bottom of the barrel" when Melroe called and told Everett to come in for work the following day. He worked for them for 20 years. We have benefited not just from the paycheck, but from all the other things we received.

Marjorie Johnson
On behalf of Everett Johnson, Manufacturing, 1963–1984

Bobcat sure changed my life . . . The growth period was the fun period. We were doing everything right, and the Melroe people didn't question me—they let me do my thing and they trusted me. It was nice to have bosses like that. They let their folks do their jobs.

Jim Johnston
Sales, 1964–1976

This truck driving was the best employment my husband ever had, so it meant financial security leading to a better standard of living for our family.

Gladys Jondahl
On behalf of Gerald Jondahl, truck driver, 1969–1981

Bobcat afforded me the opportunity to enjoy hobbies, but most of all it allowed me to create opportunities for our children and have a comfortable retirement.

Don Jorgenson
Machinist, 1978–2003

In my 17 years working with Melroe, I cannot recall one day that I dreaded going to work. I remember Paul Hotvedt saying, "Where can I go and be well paid for driving around in a new car and visiting my friends?"

Truman Kelley
District Sales, 1970–1987

It was a job where I never dreaded getting up in the morning and going to work. It was just fun to work there.

Jim Kertz
Advertising, Sales, and Marketing, 1969–1992
President and CEO, 1992–1996

Sometimes they were hard times, but always a lot of fun, and a lot of good challenges and opportunities . . . There was a lot of joy in being able to work with the Bobcat people, all trying to complete the mission of becoming Numero Uno! It was everybody's mission.

Gui Keuppens
Sales and International Sales, 1984–2001

During my 35 years with Bobcat I was always, and still am, proud to be associated with Bobcat because we were, and still are, the industry leader in innovation, design, safety, and sales worldwide . . . I feel that those who work for Bobcat are part of a special fraternity.

Eugene Kielb
Product Engineering, 1970–2005

Being a local person, it gave me a chance to stay in my hometown and work. That's almost unheard of nowadays.

Chuck Klemetson
Video productions, service/technical publications, 1958–2001

Bobcat was part of my life for 32-plus years. I planned on staying a couple of years and then leaving. A year later, I got married and the company kept on growing. I had offers to go with the copycats, but I could see no reason to as the company kept on growing—and still is. It sure took us on a ride over the years.

Roger Kudelka
Accounting, 1959–1991

There were years that we had a lot of fun . . . We worked hard, and we played hard.

Ed Larson
Manufacturing and Service, 1960–2004

I started working for Melroe in April 1957, as a welder. When the Keller brothers brought their self-propelled loader to the Melroe Company at Gwinner, they asked for some help to build the first loaders manufactured at the Melroe factory . . . It is impossible for me to express in just a few words, but pride of building a worldly product would be one of many memories. Bobcat meant a way of life that was unequaled by any other employment in our area, even in the state of North Dakota.

Donald Lloyd
Production and Service, 1957–1994

201

I came from a very large out-of-state company, so having an opportunity to come back to North Dakota and earn a living helping develop many machines was an opportunity of a lifetime for which I am grateful.

Orlan Loraas

Product Engineering, 1969–1997

My work took me to 52 foreign countries. Working with Bobcat, I received an education in worldwide business, travel, food, living, people, customs brokers, and local rules and regulations . . . Bobcat products have adapted themselves to many applications and local country requirements around the world.

Robert Lotzer

Service, 1967–1996

It was my whole life for 33 years—outside of my family. It was so good . . . It really was. It's a part of my life that I am proud of because of the people involved and the products we built.

Carman Lynnes

Engineering and Attachments, 1968–2001

Security—The opportunity to be part of a group of people that cared about you, paid you a good salary with wonderful benefits, and made you feel proud of the product ...

Marion MacArthur

Executive assistant, 1976–2001

Instilled in all of us was the art of leading people, encouraging them, and challenging their creativity so that we ALL figured out what our Bobcat customers REALLY need and want. And even more importantly, we had the WILL to succeed and the SKILL in the people, to make the Bobcat product what it continues to be today. We also had some fun along the way!

Dennis Mecklenburg

Operations, Sales, Parts, and Service,1966–1996

I worked at Melroe Company for 26 years. During this time, I watched Bobcat grow into the company it is today. We can all take pride and ownership in developing the company.

John Nadler

Loading crew foreman, 1954–1980

My work took me to New York City and to Baltimore, and I doubt I would have traveled there any other way . . . I am still proud to see a load of Bobcat machines on the road or on television or in movies. And I'm proud to tell people "Bobcat is my company."

James Officer

Traffic, 1963–2004

Bobcat was my life and my life's work. Melroe (Bobcat) was a wonderful place to spend a career. The culture was very special and work was fun. The Melroe brothers always said work should be fun and they managed to make it happen.

Orval O'Neil

Engineering, Product Management, and Sales, 1959–1998

Working at Bobcat for 38 years has been a second family and it provided me security and a good living. I've made lots of friends there and know we worked together to help make it what it is today.

Charles Orn

Assembly, 1966–2004

Every time we hear the purr of a Bobcat machine we are grateful to the Bobcat family. On our dad's grave marker is an etching of a Bobcat loader. That's how much Bobcat meant to him and our family.

Gene Paulus

(Comments provided by daughter Karen)

District sales manager, 1972–1994

That's easy: my life . . . If I were to total the amount of service that my family has contributed to the company, it would be well over 200 years.

Ginny Rader

Purchasing, 1970–2005

It's been over five years since my husband, Al Pederson, passed away. At his service, our pastor made a comment that he never wanted to buy a Bobcat machine, but Al certainly made him feel like he needed one. Bobcat was our bread and butter for 30 years and we have memories that are priceless.

Carole Pederson

On behalf of Al Pedersen, regional sales manager, 1966–1996

We were a staff, and family, of 10. We all had immense pride in "our" company. It provided me and my family with security, and I have confidence that security will be there as long as we need it.

Bernice Rasmussen

Advertising, 1976–1991

In addition to providing me with the opportunity to provide a comfortable living for my family, the Bobcat Company provided a sense of family and pride, working together to build the world's finest equipment.

Adrian "Skip" Ruhnke

Merchandising administrator, 1988–1998

Working for Bobcat is a happy memory of people who worked hard for a great company. I retired in 1995 and still miss my job and the people I worked with.

Marge Schneider
Material control supervisor, 1976–1995

Bobcat was my whole life. It made it possible for me to stay in the area and not have to move out of state to find a similar wage and benefit package.

Roger Schreiner
Manufacturing and Service, 1966–2006

We made a lot of friends, some of them lifelong.

Richard Schroeder
Sales, 1967–1989

I cannot think of any place where I could have worked and had more fun.

Jim Strand
Manufacturing, 1970–1992

The tremendous sense of collegiality among the "Bobcat members," I believe, gave the company a special edge in the market they served. Company meetings and activities seemed to be particularly designed to develop and promote this quality in its personnel.

Marcy Theede
On behalf of Fred Theede, Credit and Sales, 1962–1986

It was my whole life—it still is. I just can't say enough about the people: the people I'll never forget . . .

Mike Vig
Operations and Engineering, 1975–2004

Bobcat provided a steady, secure job that allowed me to make a good living for myself and my family in a small-town or rural-type setting. Great people to work with and for, who became friends as well as co-workers. It was a good feeling to work for the company who builds the first and best skid-steer loader ever made.

Curtis Vosberg
Product Engineering, 1968–2002

Bobcat is a life equal to your personal family, built on relationships, trust, teamwork, pride, commitment, and dedication to innovate and deliver products and services that exceed customers' expectations.

Oryn Wagner
Vice President Product Engineering, 1976–2007

It was the best company that anyone could ever hope to work for. Whether you were on the assembly line or in the marketing department, you were always informed about how things were going at Melroe. The friendliness of people was always a comment by suppliers who dealt with Melroe employees.

Al Warkenthein
Service, 1976–1995

I consider myself one of the luckiest folks in the world . . . Lucky to work for a great company that treated people with respect and had a good product we could be proud of. And lucky to work with people who were friends, not just business acquaintances.

Dale Webb
Sales, 1964–2001

We knew we had a good product, but we also knew that without the people and the distribution, it wouldn't go anywhere. That's what made Bobcat so special and so successful.

Lane Weber
Sales, 1968–2006

My husband, Jerome Wray, put in 28 years in Gwinner with Bobcat production. The benefits alone were a big item, plus the wages for this area couldn't be beat. He was proud to be a part of this company, having a good job and good people to work with, and the opportunity to move on.

Kay Wray
On behalf of Jerome Wray, Production, 1971–1991

It's not just products, it's family. My work has become pleasure. People ask me where I'd like to go on vacation, and I say, "Every day is a vacation to me."

Chin Wah Ying
International Sales, 1977–Present

Bobcat
Lore

"Fun." Whether referencing sales meetings, business trips, Bobcat Boot Camp, or just saying that working at Bobcat meant they never disliked getting up and going to work, people enjoyed themselves. That's exactly the culture that the Melroe brothers created and that countless others have carried on over the years. There are several stories that demonstrate the loose atmosphere that everyone enjoyed, and we have just a few of them to share with you. What's amazing is that people had so much fun and the company is so successful. Typically, the two don't mesh. But that's what makes Bobcat Company special, and that's what ensured people stuck around for 20, 30, and 40 years.

WORKING HARD AND PLAYING HARD . . . HALF-NORTH DAKOTAN
Gui Keuppens, with Bobcat Europe from 1984 to 2004, still recalls his first trip to North Dakota . . .

"I had to look at the map to find it, and then I had to find out how cold it was," he says. "On the plane from London to Minneapolis, my neighbor asked me where I was going, and I said 'Fargo.' The girl in

Gui Keuppens

front of me started to giggle, so I asked her what was wrong with North Dakota. My neighbor next to me answered, 'Well I was going to ask what you did wrong to be sent there.' Since that trip, I was back very frequently. In fact in my last years I was back to North Dakota about once a month . . . So I was half North Dakotan. We worked very hard, but sometimes we played. The Bobcat philosophy is work hard and play hard, and that was absolutely true. We all appreciated having fun, and I would try and get the North Dakotans to try European beer!"

CALLING AND BUZZING THE LOCAL BAR
As told by Jim Johnston
Who remembers the phone that was installed at the local Gwinner bar so company people could take calls during breaks? Or how about being "buzzed" at the bar by the Melroe plane? Jim Johnston—who started in Sales in 1964 and worked there until moving to Clark in 1976—says he had a lot to do with both. "When I was

Jim Johnston

traveling I would call in, and for a time I wasn't too familiar with the product, so I would really need to talk with someone. Nobody would be there . . . They would go for lunch at the local bar. So finally one time when I came home I had a phone installed so I could always get a hold of someone when I was on the road.

"We would also use the company airplane . . . We would fly into that little grass airstrip. There wasn't always somebody out there, so we would have to buzz the local bar with the plane when we were coming in to land. That would make the bar shake, and everyone there would know we had flown in and send somebody to come and get us!"

The Story of "Bobcat A-Go-Go"
As told by Dale Webb

If you are a long-time Bobcat employee—or even longer-time customer, chances are that you've either seen or heard about the film "Bobcat A-Go-Go." Dale Webb, retired regional sales manager, was part of the advertising department around 1967 when Ferd Froeschle and filmmaker Bill Snyder conceived and produced the legendary piece. "In those days, go-go dancers were the big thing," Webb says. "The television show *Laugh-In* was just becoming popular, too. So Ferd, who was always full of wit, decided to come up with something fun that we could use a lot at tradeshows and dealer meetings. Flint Communications was involved, too . . . In fact they helped find the go-go dancer." Product demonstrator Fez Bruns was picked to operate the machine for the film, which switches back and forth from Bobcat machine spinning and moving to the go-go girl doing her, uh, thing. "Even in those days, it wasn't that risqué," Webb says. "It was just a unique, cute, wonderful idea. People would line up at tradeshows and say, 'Hey, run that film again!'" Webb also says it came down to Bruns and another demonstrator to operate the machine. "Fez was built better for the Bobcat loader," though.

"And he had the personality and everything. He was perfect."

"During the early years that we were part of Clark Equipment Company, Orv O'Neil and I went to one of the first meetings in Buchanan, Michigan . . . All the Clark employees asked if they could see 'Bobcat A-Go-Go.' It was legendary."

"Show Me What it Can Do"
Demonstration Stories from Steve Jacobson

A key element to the success of Bobcat machines has always been the demonstration. Even today, customers want to see what the machines can do, especially when someone who knows what he is doing is at the controls. That was even more important when machines were first catching on. Steve Jacobson, an early product demonstrator and current dealer, recalls some of his most interesting showings:

"For a while, I was running the Feller Buncher in the woods industry," he says. "You could lay down about 125 trees in an hour, in a stack, with one machine. It was really amazing what it could do. I was on a demonstration once, and the people watching had this big tree, about 75 or 80 feet tall, at the bottom of a steep slope. A road was at the top of the slope. This guy said to me, 'If you can cut that tree and bring it up to the road, I'll buy two of them.' I said, 'Nothing to it.' I just cut that tree, put it over the top of the machine, and brought it up the slope and put it on the road. The guy just shook his head and said, 'A deal is a deal.' I asked, 'Do you want me to put it back?' Then I just put it over the top of the machine again and drove it back down the slope.

"Then one time I was demonstrating the 970 loader to the government. We were showing the backhoe attachment's versatility, and this guy said, 'You'll have to be able to unhook and change those in an hour.' I just looked at him and said, 'Well, I can make it a short hour.' In less than a minute, I had the backhoe off, the bucket on, and I was dumping the first load of dirt into the truck."

>> *Steve Jacobsen demonstrates the backhoe attachment on the M970 loader.*

Beach Balls Everywhere!
As told by Clint Lonbaken

One of the more talked-about practical jokes involved the "Life Is a Beach" sales promotion, says Clint Lonbaken, manager of Dealer Branding and Shared Services.

Dick Schroeder, then national accounts manager for Bobcat, headed up a series of promotional mailings to major accounts. As part of a campaign, Schroeder planned to mail all of the major accounts an uninflated beach ball along with a sales brochure promoting the new water-cooled loader. The only problem—Schroeder ordered several thousand more beach balls than he needed.

"We were pondering what to do with them. He was on the road one week, so we went out and rented an air compressor and spent an entire afternoon blowing up the beach balls," Lonbaken says.

Lonbaken and the other Bobcat employees proceeded to fill up Schroeder's 20-by-25-foot office with inflated beach balls tossing them in through a ceiling tile in the adjacent hallway.

When Schroeder returned to the office, all he could do was watch as the beach balls spilled from his office when he opened the door. "Dick had this great big smile on his face that said, 'OK, you got me, but I'm going to get you back.' And he did many times and in many ways," Lonbaken says.

>> *Holy beach balls, Dick Schroeder, where'd they all come from?*

The Show Van

As told by Paul Anderson

The Show Van, a traveling shop for preparing and maintaining equipment, has been around since 1970 and has witnessed much of Bobcat product history. It was originally created for the Road Show, a very successful introduction program for the Melroe Company skid-steer loader line and the new M970. After that product launch, The Show Van was used in the introduction of the Feller Bunchers and to help support numerous sales meetings and Bobcat Boot Camps. In addition to preparing and maintaining equipment, The Show Van is also used as a storage shed for tools, props, and building materials and as a meeting room for the crew.

Paul Anderson, global loader product manager, remembers going to an international dealer meeting in Miami, where a Sea World water ski team had been hired to perform at the outdoor boat racing site. "When we arrived the week before, we didn't have a script for how we were going to set up our program and include the ski team," he says. "While standing around the open site, Norm Selberg (our prop painter) looked up and saw a light pole by the water's edge. He said, 'We could put a crow's nest on the pole for the announcer to talk from.'"

Imagination soon took over the group. "The next thing you know, with materials from The Show Van and the local K-Mart, we had it looking like a pirate ship," Anderson says. "It was great!" The performance featured a Bobcat 443 in a treasure chest and a member of the ski team walking the plank from 14 feet in the air off a vertical-mast articulated Bobcat 2000.

The Show Van's interior walls hold years of memories because plastered on them are the names of crews and show sites from about 1975 to present. Anderson says many of those names now hold titles behind them like product representative, product manager, district manager, or even vice president. He says The Show Van provides a great starting place for new employees to become acclimated to the "Bobcat culture."

>> *A sign inside The Show Van displays the production crew roster for the 1995 dealer meeting in Orlando, Florida.*

>> *The Saw Dust Twins, Earle Benson (left) and Richard Hanson, construct sets outside The Show Van.*

>> *George Burris, Earle Benson, and Norm "Rat" Selberg (left to right) paint sets outside The Show Van.*

>> *The Show Van trailer hauled Bobcat machines, and the Road Show crew and set all over the country.*

>> *A view of the field demonstration area as Show Van crew members set up equipment and prepare for a dealer meeting.*

>> *Norm "Rat" Selberg paints a sign for the 1980 dealer meeting in Dallas, Texas.*

The Culture of Independence
As told by Jim Strand and Mike Vig

Jim Strand

One of the many reasons Bobcat has been successful is the organization's tremendous ability to be self-sufficient. Certainly Bobcat suppliers have been instrumental over the years, but there are several things Bobcat has designed and perfected, ranging from robotic cells used in manufacturing, to machine components, to equipment lines that other manufacturers outsource and brand. Sometimes it was necessary. Other times it just made sense.

"I had a deal with our purchasing department . . . If I found out we could make something better and cheaper than one of the suppliers, we'd make it in-house. If we could find a supplier who could make something better and cheaper than we could, they would make it for us," says Jim Strand, who was hired as vice president of manufacturing in 1970. "The first big one was hydraulic cylinders. We got into that in the late 70s when everything was difficult to get. Cylinder makers were falling behind, and it was hurting our production cycle badly. So we began making them just out of necessity. Interestingly, other equipment manufacturers started saying they wanted to buy our cylinders. That proved that our costs were okay, and it proved that our quality was competitive."

That same attitude led to Bobcat offering the only North America-produced compact excavator. Bobcat began working with an excavator producer in northern Japan in the late 1980s. The idea was that Bobcat would learn how to produce the machine efficiently and bring that process back to the United States. "Work ethic is a phrase that's been overused, but it applies to the people of North Dakota," says Mike Vig, who started in 1975 and became vice president of engineering in 1997. "North Dakota people don't want to lose. You give them a challenge, and they're up for it. We'd tell our employees that we were going to send something overseas and see what it costs. They would usually say, 'Give it back to us and we can match that cost. We'll figure out how to do it.' And they generally always did. We selected a company in Japan who was willing to talk with us and pass on knowledge, so we could eventually produce the units ourselves. They were making compact excavators for various companies but they didn't actually sell into the market. So they were willing to help with the design and share information with our engineers so we could match it to our standards and processes." Thus, Bobcat compact excavators manufactured at the Bismarck facility became the first produced in the United States in 1989. And, likewise, Bobcat continues to manufacture many components for machines that other manufacturers typically buy.

209

Dealer Channel

One major reason Bobcat is a leader in the design, manufacture, marketing, and distribution of compact equipment particularly involves distribution. Without the best dealers in the industry, Bobcat would have no means to locally promote, demonstrate, and sell products. And over the years, Bobcat has recognized this as a partnership. Many individuals who contributed to this book commented on how—dating back to the Melroe Manufacturing Company—dealers were considered part of the family. From setting up the first Bobcat dealers during the late 1950s and early 1960s, to organizing the Dealer Advisory Council (D.A.C.) and creating "Bobcat of . . . " locations, the philosophy remained the same. Dealers were not just a channel; they were part of the organization, and a critical part at that. So as individuals recall the opportunities that arose working for and with Bobcat, for many of the dealers it was an opportunity to create a successful, self-sustained business. It is mostly because many of them were successful that Bobcat has become the global brand it is today. This section celebrates all Bobcat dealers . . . those who are in their second and third generations, as well as those who have just joined the family.

The black-and-white photo was taken in 1971 as Clark Equipment Australia Pty. Limited assumed full responsibility for marketing Bobcat equipment Down Under. The celebratory shot appeared on the cover of the organization's publication, Lift and Shift. The same group (now the team at Bobcat Australia) reenacted the famous picture in 2006.

THE "BOBCAT OF . . ." STORY

Doug Freitag—a Bobcat veteran who began as a demonstrator and worked his way up to vice president of sales and marketing before retiring in 2004—calls his involvement in furthering the development of the "Bobcat of" dealerships his single biggest accomplishment at Bobcat. His part began during the mid-1970s, when there was already some energy behind the creation of the first "Bobcat of . . . " dealerships, he says. There were two "Bobcat of . . . " locations in the southern territory where Freitag served as a district manager. He started learning firsthand the value of more specialization for a dealer, and a separate, focused operation for parts, service and, especially, sales. By the late 1970s, Freitag and others believed there was a big enough market to move the cause forward even more, and Bobcat began to fund the program and put the right people in place to make it happen. He recalls that a couple of "rougher business cycles were pretty hard on those guys." But, everyone was learning that Bobcat had to move to a higher plane with dealers and give them financial management and guidance necessary to get through downturns. The number of "Bobcat of . . . " operations in Freitag's territory continued to grow, and the same was happening in areas around his. He recognized the opportunities for cross-sharing and training. All the salespeople thought the same way, he says. "If they don't sell Bobcat machines each day, they don't eat, and that was key," he says. "We knew we had to get them as dependent on us as we are on them." With help from the early D.A.C., Bobcat began creating

standards for "Bobcat of . . ." dealers and providing routine consultation on business practices. "Then we really started to find the synergies of two groups of people with a common understanding and a common mission," he says. "We focused on getting one thing done for the benefit of both." In 1978, Freitag headed to Fargo to take a corporate position and started working with the executive management team, who supported the continuation of driving this philosophy. Then things really took off. The economy was robust coming out of the downturn, Freitag says, so it was a great time for dealers to step out and make the commitment. "Everyone in Fargo and Gwinner became aware of how much easier, fun, profitable, and productive it was to work with "Bobcat of . . ." dealers, he says. "That was the period that the entire organization committed themselves and saw the future."

Doug Freitag

A cartoon of Doug Freitag carrying a bag of cash while swinging on a vine through the jungle is just one of many dealer promotions that made Freitag a well-known face among Bobcat dealers. Freitag was instrumental in furthering the development of the "Bobcat of" dealerships during the 1970s and 1980s. And in those beginning years, he often used his own name and face in promotions to spark dealers' excitement, thus becoming a character in his own right.

>> An internal dealer promotion featuring Jim Brust, Roger Fischer, and Doug Freitag (left to right) photographed in the Bonanzaville historical museum complex in West Fargo, North Dakota.

>> Port-A-Feeder Sales Co., Mandan, North Dakota.

>> The Dealer Advisory Council presents a plaque to Bobcat Vice President of Sales Jim Johnston (from left: Del Husfeldt, Jim Johnston, Ed Hammond, and Jack Arsenault).

>> Daniel Dierdorf, a former NFL football player and president of Fox Pools of St. Louis Inc., poses with his Bobcat skid-steer loader as part of a dealer's ad campaign.

>> Feller Dealer, Germany 1981.

>> Pete Roble, Bobcat Vice President of international marketing, dines with German dealers at a dealer banquet.

>> Jim Kertz (far right) and his staff at the European offices, 1979.

>> *Several just-trained salespeople celebrate graduation outside the Swedish dealership.*

>> *Howard Bernstein, Atlas Lift Trucks, finds Bobcat working in Jerusalem.*

>> *Staff from the Vangaever dealership presented the Top Dealership award by Jim Kertz.*

Letter from Harry Rawley, Valley Implement Sales, Inc.

I became a dealer for Bobcat in December 1964 . . . I am retired and my three sons—Dennis, Doug, and Rick—now operate the business.

My relationship with Bobcat got off to a rocky start. I had ordered three machines when I signed the contract—two 444 models and one 500 model. I demonstrated these machines but just couldn't get anyone to buy the first one. Most of our customers at that time were farmers. They liked the machine and what it could do, but just would not spend the money to buy one. So I decided to cancel my contract. Jim Johnston with Melroe flew to Virginia to try and convince me to change my mind, but he wasn't successful. There was a clause in the contract that allowed either party to cancel, and Melroe would repurchase the machines in inventory, provided they were new and unused. It just so happened that all three of our machines had been demonstrated and had some hours. Jim agreed that the company would still take them back, but at a reduced price. We negotiated the amount of the reduction, and Jim proposed one amount but I thought another amount. Finally, Jim said, "Let's flip a coin to determine which figure to use." I lost (I still think he used a two-headed coin). Jim assured me it would be at least a month before he could have the machines picked up, so he suggested that I go back to some of the people who I had demonstrated to and offer to sell them at dealer cost to save me from losing the buy-back reduction. I did what he suggested, and I sold all three units within a month. Then I called Jim and told him to send me more machines. Bobcat proved to me during this time that they took care of their dealers and their customers. They have proved it any number of times in the past 42 years, and Bobcat has always been one of the best suppliers with whom we do business.

216

>> *Sid Duhon (left) of Duhon Machinery Co. Inc. with Cliff Melroe at the 1970 dealer meeting in Chandler, Arizona.*

>> *Harry Newton and Dick Schmidtz of Atlas Material Handling, along with his wife, Mary, chat with Cliff Melroe (second from left) at the 1970 dealer meeting in Chandler, Arizona.*

>> Models of Bobcat compact equipment are arranged and displayed for a toy brochure. Feland says this photo was especially challenging because it had to be shot at a specific angle in order to maintain its narrowness. Once complete, the art department filled the open spaces with text.

>> A Bobcat 753 skid-steer loader dumps a load of sand at dusk with its headlights glowing. This photo was taken in the early 1990s for a literature piece on accessories. Feland says he likes the photo's lighting and how it captures the sand slowing falling from the bucket.

>> A Toolcat 5600 utility work machine with a mower attachment cuts grass and mulches leaves along the fence of a horse ranch in fall 2006. Feland says he chose this photo as a favorite because he likes how the fence and trees help frame the machine.

>> A Bobcat 753 skid-steer loader dumps dirt and sand in a desert area just east of Phoenix with Superstition Mountain in the background. The beautiful scenery put this photo on the cover of WorkSaver magazine and makes it a Feland favorite.

>> A Toolcat 5600 utility work machine with a snowblower attachment clears several inches of snow from a commercial parking lot in Fargo. This was taken following a snowstorm in winter 2004. The only way to take good snow photos is on a clear, sunny day because snow isn't distinguishable in photos taken on cloudy days, Feland says.

>> For the introduction of the new Bobcat Farmboy skid-steer loader, Feland took this photo of Bobcat employee Lynn Roesler and his wife at North Dakota State University. Feland's love of horses makes this one of his favorites.

>> A Spra-Coupe sprays an Alabama cotton field on a hot, humid day. Bobcat purchased the Spra-Coupe in 1973 and manufactured the machines until it sold the line 1998. Growing up as a farm boy, Feland says he likes this photo because he can relate to spraying crops.

>> A Bobcat wheel saw attachment on a Bobcat 853 skid-steer loader lowers to slice through an asphalt parking lot in Gwinner, North Dakota. The angle of the wheel saw attachment coming down on the asphalt makes this a Feland favorite.

Bobcat

Oh' the places we've been . . .

229

(Above) New Bobcat owners are proud of their acquisition in the United Arab Emirates.

(Top right) Dworp was the headquarters for Bobcat Europe in 1970s.

(Right) A Bobcat loader is demonstrated at the Zimbabwe Fair.

>> Preben Lange of the Copenhagen dealership.

>> Bobcat loader at a prehistoric tourist attraction.

>> A Bobcat loader at work in Syria.

>> The local Bobcat dealership sponsored a ladies' basketball team in Sweden during the 1970s.

230

>> Southern Mechanical—a Bobcat dealer in England— was chief sponsor of a raceboat on the European circuit.

>> A Bobcat loader rides up the mountains of Sweden.

>> A Bobcat loader in South Africa carries sugar cane.

>> Bobcat Loaders on the beach in Finland.

>> Bobcat loader getting dirty in Wahpeton, North Dakota.

>> Bobcat fans in Afghanistan.

231

>> Not your everyday work site in New Salem North Dakota.

>> A Bobcat loader goes head to head with a giant Clark Michigan wheel loader in Michigan.

BOBCAT

ALL-WHEEL STEER LOADERS

ARTICULATED LOADERS

A220
2001–2003

A300
2002–Present

1600
1983–1993

2000
1981–1987

2400
1988–1991

2410
1991–1995

COMPACT EXCAVATORS

56
1986–1989

76
1986–1989

100
1986–1989

116
1986–1989

130
1987–1989

220
1990–1993

COMPACT EXCAVATORS

225
1990–1993

231
1990–1993

316
2003–Present

319
2005–Present

320
1996–Present

322
1999–2005

LOADER BACKHOE

B300
2002–2006

MINI TRACK LOADERS

MT50
2002–2003

MT52
2003–Present

MINI TRACK LOADERS

MT55
2004–Present

SKID-STEER LOADER

310
1977–1983

313
1978–1983

SKID-STEER LOADERS

440
1983–1986

Farmboy
1985–1986

440B
1986–1995

443
1983–1994

443B
1993–1994

450
1994–1998

SKID-STEER LOADERS

453
1994–2001

463
2000–Present

520
1976–1977

530
1977–1982

533
1976–1982

540
1981–1986

SKID-STEER LOADERS

542B
1988–1993

543
1981–1994

543B
1993–1994

553
1994–2007

630
1977–1982

631
1977–1982

SKID-STEER LOADERS

632
1977–1982

641
1981–1991

642
1981–1986

642B
1986–1992

643
1981–1992

645
1992–1994

SKID-STEER LOADERS

653
1995–1997

720
1975–1979

721
1975–1979

722
1976–1979

730
1978–1980

731
1978–1982

SKID-STEER LOADERS

732
1978–1982

741
1981–1991

742
1981–1991

742B
1991–1995

743
1981–1991

743B
1990–1995

SKID-STEER LOADERS

743DS
1983–1991

751
1995–2000

753
1990–2003

753L
1993-1994

763
1994–2003

7753
1991–1994

SKID-STEER LOADERS

773
1994–2002

773 Turbo
1999–2002

773 Turbo 500K Edition
2001–2002

825
1975–1983

843
1981–1992

843B
1990–1992

SKID-STEER LOADERS

853
1990–1996

863
1996–2003

873
1995–2002

883
2001–2002

943
1985–1994

953
1994–1997

SKID-STEER LOADERS

963
1997–2002

974
1975–1990

975
1974–1990

980
1986–1994

M60 3-Wheel Loader
1958–1959

M200 3-Wheel Loader
1959–1962

SKID-STEER LOADERS

M371
1971–1977

M400
1960–1962

M440
1962–1962

M444
1963–1972

M500
1964–1972

M500E
1964–1972

SKID-STEER LOADERS

M600
1967–1975

M500E / M600E
1964–1978

M610
1972–1982

M611
1975–1978

M620
1975–1976

M700
1973–1976

SKID-STEER LOADERS

M970
1970–1975

S130
2003–Present

S150
2003–Present

S160
2003–Present

S175
2002–Present

S185
2002–Present

SKID-STEER LOADERS

S205
2004–Present

S220
2003–Present

S250
2002–Present

S300
2002–Present

S330
2006–Present

TELESCOPIC HANDLERS

T2556＊
1998–Present

TELESCOPIC HANDLERS

T2566*
1998–Present

T3571*
2004–Present

T35100*
2006–Present

T35120*
2004–Present

T40140*
1999–Present

T40170*
2003–Present

* International models
† North American models

254

TELESCOPIC HANDLERS

V416†
2007–Present

V518†
2001–Present

V623†
2001–2004

V638†
2006–Present

V723†
2004–Present

TRENCHERS

T108
1986–1988

TRENCHERS

T114
1986–1987

T116
1987–1992

T135
1987–1989

T136
1986–1989

T208
1988–1991

T209
1991–1992

TRENCHERS

2021
1989–1991

3022
1989–1991

3023
1989–1992

TOOLCAT UTILITY WORK MACHINE

5600
2002–Present

UTILITY VEHICLES

2100
2002–Present

2100S
2003–2006

UTILITY VEHICLES

2200
2004–Present

2200S
2006–Present

2300
2006–Present

VERTICAL MAST MACHINES

M444
1963–1972

M500
1964–1972

M600
1967–1975

VERTICAL MAST MACHINES

2000 RTF
1982–1985

FELLER BUNCHERS

M174 prototype
1973–1973

1074
1975–1978

FELLER BUNCHERS

1075
1975–1978

1080
1979–1987

1213
1985–1986

Acknowledgements

Scores of individuals who dedicated themselves, and in some cases, their entire careers, to Bobcat were instrumental in the development of this book. Without them, the Bobcat story—told or untold—would not have been. Certainly because of these remarkable people, we are able to finally put down on paper an account that has meant so much to so many.

260

Special thanks to:
Ernie Feland, Bobcat Company photographer of 37 years, for his historical guidance and research, not to mention his extraordinary photography that always deserves credit.

Sylvan Melroe, who continues to preserve the Melroe family legacy, for providing historical material for the book, and for confirming facts and dates throughout the editing process. We are also grateful to **Cliff Melroe** and **Eugene Dahl**, who kindly gave their time as well.

Leroy Anderson, who in his role as Bobcat Company historian, has dreamed for many years of a book that would preserve the rich Bobcat story for generations to come, and worked for many months to help bring it to fruition.

Cyril and **Louis Keller**, who were of course responsible for developing the first loader and who were kind enough to share their stories and recollections through personal interviews.

Clint Lonbaken, **Paul Anderson**, and others at Bobcat Company today, who diligently helped confirm facts and history. Also, **Tom Ihringer**, **Jim Plasynski**, and **Gary Hornbacher**, whose painstaking review of the manuscript and layouts provided accuracy and consistency in telling the Bobcat story.

Donovan Kolness of Flint Communications, who provided a wonderful historical marketing perspective, and who literally opened his doors and files to share vintage Bobcat materials that helped illustrate the story.

Joe Keller, his sister **Marilyn Loegering**, and the entire **Keller family** for use of photographs and historical information from their private archives.

The countless other individuals around the world who also gave interviews and anecdotes that brought this story to life for common Bobcat enthusiasts, retirees, dealers, employees, and family members. Their recollections were used throughout the book and for background. We appreciate these individuals' time and passion for Bobcat Company and this project.

Finally, thanks to the teams at Two Rivers Marketing and Flint Communications—**Jennifer Boling**, **Tara Deering-Hansen**, **Jeff White**, and **Casey Gregerson** and others—who provided production support and guidance to MBI throughout the process, and who worked on all materials for the special 50th Anniversary edition.

Epilogue

PRIDE OF NORTH DAKOTA

Employees past and present who nurtured the Bobcat skid-steer loader describe their machine's impact on the world best. "What the successful guys appreciated," former engineering vice president Jim Bauer said, "is that the skid-steer loader wasn't a machine, it was a man amplifier, a 'man-replacer.' Back in the '60s, we said that if you sold a contractor a loader, he could replace 15 people. Where we used to use wheelbarrows and shovels, now you use a Bobcat skid-steer loader. It's a marvelous machine and the world is a lot better off with it than it was without it."

The machine made work easier—and invariably, it made the company proud to be a part of its story.

"I didn't go to college," said dealer and former demonstrator Steve Jacobsen. "I started right after school. The people that were there all the years I was there were just kind. Everybody looked out for everybody. I got an education that I never would have had in any college. If the Melroe boys were here today and started another company, I'd go to work for them," he said.

Retired video producer Chuck Klemetson attributed the Bobcat success story to "the pride of working with something you figured would really take off—the pride of it being a small company in a rural state that is actually making good. It would give us a lot

of pride when we would see these things show up on newsreels," he recalled.

"It's the people that have made this company," says photographer Ernie Feland, "hard work and teamwork. I know whenever I see Bobcat equipment on the jobsite, on a trailer going down the highway or a Bobcat truck loaded with machines going down the interstate, I'll feel proud to have worked for such a great company."

Index

Bobcat models
2000 articulated loader, 80, 154, 226
2000 rough terrain forklift (RTF), 154
2100 utility vehicle, 169
2200 utility vehicle, 183
2300 utility vehicle, 183
40-Series loaders, 139
430 compact excavator, 165, 182
435 ZHS , compact excavator, 182
440B skid-steer loader, 141
442 compact excavator, 144
520 B-series, 114
542 skid-steer loader, 141
642 skid-steer loader, 141
643 skid-steer loader, 116
731 skid-steer loader, 90
743 skid-steer loader, 136, 137, 139
751 F-series skid-steer loader, 188
753 skid-steer loader, 226, 227
763 skid-steer loader, 160
773 Turbo skid-steer loader, 145, 167
825 skid-steer loader, 115
843 skid-steer loader, 137, 141
843H skid-steer loader, 141
853 skid-steer loader, 137, 228
864 compact track loader, 120
873 skid-steer loader, 159
943 skid-steer loader, 97, 141
963 skid-steer loader, 226
980 skid-steer loader, 139, 141, 182
A220 all-wheel steer loader, 182
A300 all-wheel steer loader, 160, 161, 225
B-series, 110, 112, 114, 115
Farmboy skid-steer loader, 139, 141
Harroweeder, 10, 11, 15, 21, 26, 29, 32, 40, 192
M200 3-wheel loader, 22, 24, 26, 31, 51
M371 "Mini Bob" skid-steer loader, 97–101, 110, 115, 182, 189
M400 skid-steer loader, 8, 25, 26, 31, 51, 182

M440 skid-steer loader, 25, 29–31, 48, 49, 51, 65
M444 skid-steer loader, 46, 50, 64, 76
M500 skid-steer loader, 49, 64, 68, 76, 96, 116
M500E skid-steer loader, 50, 77
M60 Self-Propelled Loader, 18, 21–24, 27, 28, 31, 51
M600 skid-steer loader, 60, 73, 76, 103, 111, 117, 136, 137, 182, 225
M600E skid-steer loader, 77
M610 dairy special, 89
M610 skid-steer loader, 64, 68, 81, 87, 108, 110, 114, 116, 137, 159
M700 hydrostatic skid-steer loader, 78
M970 "Big Bob" skid-steer loader, 97–101, 103, 108–110, 115, 117, 182, 206, 208, 225
Moldboard plow, 32
MT52 mini track loader, 182
MT55 mini track loader, 165
S130 skid-steer loader, 170
S175 skid-steer loader, 170
S250 skid-steer loader, 161
S300 skid-steer loader, 149
Skid-steer loader, 28–30, 45, 52
Spra-Coupe, *see* Kirschmann, Spra-Coupe
T108 trencher, 142
T114 trencher, 142
T136 trencher, 142
T250 compact track loader, 163
T300 compact track loader, 165, 225
Toolcat 5600 utility work machine, 147, 153, 161, 165, 166, 168, 182, 183, 227, 228
Uniloader, 96, 97
VersaHandler telescopic tool carrier, 166
Windrow pickup, 12–15, 21, 26, 29, 32, 40, 67

Other index
Akers, Wyatt, 217
Albright, Larry, 198
Alme, Norman, 198
Anderson, Leroy, 97, 193, 260
Anderson, Paul, 102, 103, 124, 170, 174, 198, 208, 260

262

Arsenault, Jack, 213, 217
Attachments, 102, 103, 124, 125
    backhoe, 101
    breaker, 103
    broom, 68
    bucket, 92
    feller buncher, 106, 103
    rockhound, 103

Bauer, Jim, 50, 99, 100, 102, 110, 112, 114, 261
Beckstrom, Harold, 198
Benson, Earle, 208
Benson, Ruby, 198
Bernstein, Howard, 215
Bickett, Lynn, 28, 29
Bliven family, 176, 177
Bobcat Interlock Control System (BICS), 182, 183
Bobcat Operation Sensing System (BOSS), 182
Bob-Tach system, 102, 103, 147, 182
Bolduc, Nate, 179
Boling, Jennifer, 260
Borke, Bud, 47, 199, 220
Bosch, Robbie, 151
Brandt, Alvin, 132
Brinkmeyer, Paul, 131
Brown, Dorene, 199
Brown, Jerry, 32
Brust, Jim, 62, 199, 212
Burdick, Quentin, 133
Burgess, Lionel, 218
Burris, George, 208

Christianson, Anton, 21, 38
Clark Equipment Company, buyout, 72–75, 78, 79, 178
Colby, LaVerne, 134
Cook, Roger, 137
Cox, Tim, 217
Cuypers, Paul, 199

Dahl, Eugene R., 13, 16, 36–38, 50, 51, 65, 71, 83, 86, 199, 260
Dahl, Evelyn "Evie," 12, 13, 36, 38
Deering-Hansen, Tara, 260
Dierdorf, Daniel, 213
Dorgan, Byron, 133
Duhon, Sid, 216
Duhon, Sid, 61

Enervold, Enne, 199

Farmhand company, 19, 22
Feland, Ernie, 224–228, 260, 261
Fischer, Kevin, 170
Fischer, Paul, 150
Fischer, Roger, 57, 62, 92, 154, 155, 199, 212
Flint Communications, 63, 93, 186, 205
Flint, Harold, 63
Ford, Harrison, 168
Fouquette, Frank, 57
Fowler, Jack, 199
Freitag, Doug, 199, 211, 212

Froeschle, Fred, 53, 155, 191, 205

Gackle, Earle, 199
Geiger, Jonathan, 168
Gerriets, Dick, 199
Glas, Bob, 32
Gould, Brown & Bickett, 28
Granlund, Royce, 57
Green, Al, 221
Gregerson, Casey, 260
Griggs, John, 199
Grosz, Bernice, 199
Gunsch, Emil, 199
Gysler Manufacturing, 110

Halvorson, Eugene, 199
Hammond, Ed, 213, 217
Hansen, Doreen, 199
Hanson, Galen, 200
Hanson, Richard, 200, 208
Hebert, Becky, 200
HED Corp., 103
Hegle, Gerald, 200
Hein, Fred, 110, 200
Henline, John, 99, 131, 200
Hoffman, Greg, 217
Hoge, Chuck, 166, 200
Holmberg, Dave, 217
Holmstrom, Allen, 200
Hombacher, Gary, 260
Hopewell, Carolyn, 200
Hotvedt, Paul, 63
Hough Equipment Company, 27
    Payloader, 54
Husfeldt, Del, 213

Ihringer, Tom, 260
Immer, Scott, 223
Ingersoll-Rand Company, acquisition by, 145, 153, 154, 179
IntelliTrack drive system, 183
Irwin, Gordon, 23, 24, 29, 200

Jacobsen, Steve, 35, 75, 101, 206, 261
Jacobson, Carolyn, 200
Janssen, Robert, 200
Jensen, Max, 201
Johndahl, Gladys, 201
Johnson, Marjorie, 201
Johnston, Jim, 74, 201, 204, 213
Jorgenson, Don, 201

Keller Manufacturing, 17, 20, 21
    loader, 18–22, 51, 180, 182
Keller, Cyril, 10, 17, 19–24, 26, 27, 31, 33, 50, 73, 99, 106, 108, 157, 166, 260
Keller, Joe, 260
Keller, Louis, 10, 17, 21, 23–25, 33, 97–99, 106, 108, 157, 166, 260
Kelley, Truman, 201
Kertz, Jim, 38, 78, 79, 83, 92, 135, 139, 191, 201, 214, 215
Keuppens, Gui, 201, 204
Kielb, Eugene, 201

Kirschmann, 86
  Spra-Coupe, 83, 86, 108, 143, 149, 154, 228
Klappersack, Carol, 168
Klemetson, Chuck, 201, 261
Klumker, Louis and Steve, 136, 137
Kolness, Donovan, 93, 186, 260
Kudelka, Roger, 201

Ladine, Ralph, 29
Landby, John, 52, 54, 73
Lange, Preben, 230
Lano, Hauser, 217
Larson, Ed, 8, 57, 92, 96, 97, 201
Leppo, Glenn, 217
Lloyd, Donald, 32, 201
Loegering, Marilyn, 260
Lonbaken, Clint, 81, 207, 221, 260
Loraas, Orlan, 202
Lotzer, Robert, 57, 202
Loula, Bob, 217
Luff & Smith, 67, 100

Lynnes, Carman, 62, 87, 124, 126, 127, 129, 202, 221
MacArthur, Marion, 202
Mader, Ken, 167
Manikkam, Ram, 218
Manke, Bob, 220
Mansfield, Mike, 133
McCullough, Bob, 48
McFarland, Ronnie, 95
McIntyre, Richard, 131
Mecklenburg, Dennis, 32, 202
Melroe Manufacturing Company, founding, 8
Melroe, Clifford E., 12, 14, 16, 23–25, 33, 36–39, 47, 51, 54, 57, 61,
  71, 73, 74, 78, 82, 83, 101, 124, 166, 178, 216, 217, 260
Melroe, Edward Gideon "E. G.," 9–16, 22, 29, 32, 37, 67, 178
Melroe, Irving L., 12, 14, 16, 22, 25, 29, 37, 38, 47, 63, 72, 166, 178
Melroe, Lester W. "Les," 12, 14, 16, 21, 25, 36–38, 47, 65, 72, 83,
  98, 178, 180
Melroe, Roger, 12, 14, 16, 17, 25, 37, 38, 47, 62, 65, 71, 72, 74, 82, 178
Melroe, Sig, 11, 38
Melroe, Sylvan, 22, 23, 25, 26, 28, 29, 36, 51, 52, 54, 56, 63, 68, 87,
  102, 106, 260
Michels, Al, 81
Moore, Jim, 87
Museums, 180, 181

Nadler, John, 202
Newton, Harry, 216

O'Neil, Orval, 29, 49–51, 96, 100, 124, 154, 202, 205
Officer, James, 202
Orn, Charles, 202
Orr, Dick, 48

Paczkowski, Lyle, 223
Paul, Cherie, 63
Paulus, Gene, 202
Pederson, Al, 56, 220
Pederson, Carole, 202
Pennington, Ty, 176
Phebus, Bill, 217

Phillips, Bert, 74, 82, 83
Plasynski, Jim, 260

Rader, Ginny, 202
RapidLink system, 166, 183
Rardin, Donn, 222
Rasmussen, Bernice, 202
Rawley, Harry, 216
Riebe, Grover, 88, 90, 123, 126, 132–135, 155, 156
Rinehardt, Jim, 127, 129
Roble, Pete, 214
Rouse, Henry, 218
Ruhnke, Adrian "Skip," 202

Salberg, Darrel, 132
Scheiderer, Rudy, 150
Schillinger, Ed, 17, 21
Schirmer, Walter, 73, 75
Schmidtz, Dick, 216
Schneider, Marge, 203
Schreiner, Roger, 203
Schroeder, Richard, 203, 207
Selberg, Norm "Rat," 208, 209
Snyder, William D. E. "Bill," 72
Spolum, Robert N., 39, 40, 43, 47, 48, 50, 71–75, 78, 86, 100, 101,
  105, 106, 108, 113, 127, 129–131, 133–135
Stansfield, Reg, 222
Strand, Jim, 110, 129, 203, 209

Theede, Fred, 220
Theede, Marcy, 203, 220
Toyo Umpanki, 105, 122, 126
Trade shows, 172, 173

U.S. Steel, 11, 15

Vangaever, Dries, 150
Velo, Eddie, 10, 18–21, 29, 33, 180
Vig, Mike, 203, 209
Vollmers, Wally, 131
Vosberg, Curtis, 203

Wagner, Oryn, 203
Wahl, Ed, 47
Wallace, Gus, 99
Waloch, Squirt, 73
Walsh, John P., 219
Warkenthein, Al, 203
Webb, Dale, 32, 203, 205
Weber, Lane, 203
White, Jeff, 260
White, Roger, 96
Wicklein, John, 47
Wohlwend, Don, 103
Woods, Bob, 218
WorkSaver, 193–197
Wray, Kay, 203

Yengst, Charles, 159
Ying, Chin Wah, 203